D0722710

CHOCOLATOLOGY

Chocolate's Fantastical Lore, Bittersweet History, & Delicious (Vegan) Recipes

ANGEL YORK AND DARIN WICK
ILLUSTRATED BY CAT CALLAWAY

MICROCOSM PUBLISHING
PORTLAND, OR

CHOCOLATOLOGY

CHOCOLATE'S FANTASTICAL LORE, BITTERSWEET HISTORY, & DELICIOUS (VEGAN) RECIPES

Angel York & Darin Wick, 2018
This Edition © Microcosm Publishing, 2018
Scripting by Nina Sandelin Umont, SandelinDesigns.com
Pages 67, 72-75, 80, 89-90, 92-93, 97, 104, 109, 111-112, 117, 119, 136, 143-145, 165, 168-169, endpapers, with food prepation by Jeri Cain Rossi and photos by Greg Clarke, CanteenPhoto.com
Pages 51, 55-56, 63, 65, 68, 70, 114-115, 120, 128-129, 158, 162, with photos by Brandie Bloggins, 2flirtygirlsandajuicer.com
Illustrated by Cat Callaway

Microcosm Publishing
2752 N Williams Ave.
Portland, OR 97227
www.microcosmpublishing.com
(503) 799-2698

ISBN 978-1-62106-289-9
This is Microcosm #198
First edition (January 10, 2018) 5,000 copies

Library of Congress Cataloging-in-Publication Data

Names: York, Angel, author. | Wick, Darin, author. | Callaway, Cat, illustrator.
Title: Chocolatology : its fantastical lore, bittersweet history, & delicious (vegan) recipes / Angel York & Darin Wick ; illustrated by Cat Callaway.
Description: First edition. | Portland, OR : Microcosm Publishing, [2018] | Includes bibliographical references and index.
Identifiers: LCCN 2017034398 | ISBN 9781621062899 (paper-over-board)
Subjects: LCSH: Cooking (Chocolate) | Vegan cooking. | LCGFT: Cookbooks.
Classification: LCC TX767.C5 Y67 2018 | DDC 641.6/374--dc23

LC record available at https://lccn.loc.gov/2017034398

MICROCOSM · PUBLISHING

Microcosm Publishing is Portland's most diversified publishing house and distributor with a focus on the colorful, authentic, and empowering. Our books and zines have put your power in your hands since 1996, equipping readers to make positive changes in their lives and in the world around them. Microcosm emphasizes skill-building, showing hidden histories, and fostering creativity through challenging conventional publishing wisdom with books and bookettes about DIY skills, food, bicycling, gender, self-care, and social justice. What was once a distro and record label was started by Joe Biel in his bedroom and has become among the oldest independent publishing houses in Portland, OR. We are a politically moderate, centrist publisher in a world that has inched to the right for the past 80 years.

If you bought this on Amazon, I'm so sorry. You could have gotten it cheaper and supported a small, independent publisher at MicrocosmPublishing.com

Global labor conditions are bad, and our roots in industrial Cleveland in the 70s and 80s makes us appreciate the need to treat workers right. Therefore, our books are MADE IN THE USA and printed on post-consumer paper.

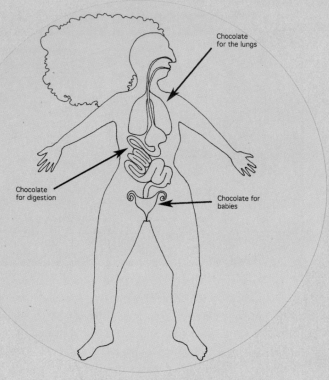

Chocolate
for the lungs

Chocolate
for digestion

Chocolate for
babies

By the wise and Moderate use whereof,
Health is preserved, Sickness
Diverted, and Cured, especially the
Plague of the Guts; vulgarly called
The New Disease; Fluxes, Consumptions,
& Coughs of the Lungs, with sundry
other desperate Diseases. By it
also, Conception is Caused,
the Birth Hastened and
facilitated, Beauty
Gain'd and continued.

Antonio Colmenero de Ledesma (1631)
from *Chocolate: or, An Indian Drinke*
translated by James Wadsworth (1652)

∽ TABLE OF CONTENTS ∽

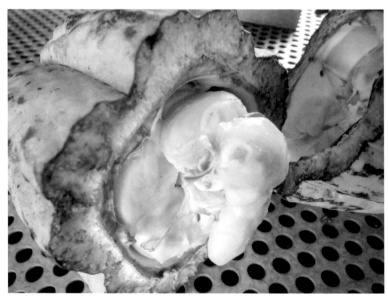

A BRIEF HISTORY OF CHOCOLATE

---

*W*e'd like to start by acknowledging that the history of chocolate as we've come to understand it through our research—and therefore also this chapter—is mostly a history of Mesoamerica and of Eurocentric colonialism. We've included some non-chocolate events to give a sense of what was happening around the world throughout the history of chocolate.

Around the turn of the new millennium, newspapers throughout the world ran headlines about child slavery in chocolate production. It was treated as a startling revelation—major governments convened task forces while human rights groups put out press releases. But slavery isn't new or surprising in the chocolate industry. It can be traced from contemporary child labor back to colonial African plantations, from the Spanish colonization of South America to Aztec tribute states—at least seven thousand years of forced labor. Most chocolate has always been and continues to be a product of slavery and economic inequality.

MESOAMERICA: FROM THE OLMECS TO THE TRIANGLE TRADE

Cacao is called the food of the gods, and for much of its history it has also been the food of the elite. While it may have been a staple for the Olmec or pre-Olmec peoples who originally cultivated it in Central America and the Amazon basin, we have no solid evidence. By the time of the first written records—Classic Maya burial inscriptions from 1000 CE or earlier—chocolate was reserved for ceremonial occasions, or for the wealthy.

When Hernán Cortés took over Tenochtitlan, the Aztec capital, Aztec law and custom had put similar limits of their supply. The rest came

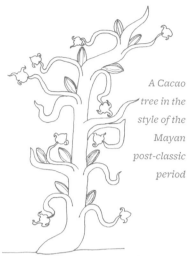

A Cacao tree in the style of the Mayan post-classic period

as tribute on chocolate consumption. The Aztecs were unable to grow cacao near their capital because of its latitude, so they relied on trade for some from those conquered in battle—a sort of feudal arrangement.

The Spaniards at first relied on the same network of trade and tribute established by the Aztecs to provide their cacao. That wasn't sustainable in the long run, with the Spanish appetite for chocolate growing and native Americans decimated by invasion and disease. Cacao supply eventually dropped

PRE-COLUMBIAN AMERICA: A CHOCOLATE TIMELINE

Cacao probably originated in the Amazon basin, somewhere around Ecuador, and was spread—possibly by humans—to the Soconusco region of Mexico and Guatemala.

1900 BCE: The pre-Olmec Mokaya people are the first society that we know consumed chocolate.

1400 BCE: First evidence of a fermented alcoholic beverage made with cacao pulp.

1250 BCE: *The Olmec civilization reaches its first peak at San Lorenzo around the time of the events in Mediterranean Europe that inspired the Iliad and Odyssey.*

1000 BCE: Mayan peoples move from mountains and high plains into the Yucatán Peninsula and Guatemalan lowlands, where they are able to cultivate cacao.

Mayan and Aztec hot chocolate was frothed by pouring it back and forth between two vessels. The resulting foam was a particular delicacy.

630-612 BCE: Sappho the poet is born somewhere in this time period on the Greek island of Lesbos. "Love shook my heart / Like the wind on the mountain / Troubling the oak-trees."

250: Mayan society enters its "Classic period" in the Petén lowlands of Guatemala, comparable to ancient Greece or Renaissance Italy.

613: Mayan civilization is at its peak. Meanwhile, on the other side of the world, the prophet Muhammad begins to preach about visions he receives, which will become the basis of Islam.

770: Cacao is imported to what is now known as Utah.

800: The Classic Maya Collapse occurs, when major cities at the center of the Mayan region become uninhabitable due to environmental degradation and overpopulation. The populace flees south to the highlands and north to the Yucatán, which is experiencing a renaissance of its own. Coastal Mayan traders and cacao growers in the Chontalpa region thrive as well, likely monopolizing trade with the Valley of Mexico.

and prices jumped. Former conquistadors were running out of American empires to conquer and saw a new opportunity. They established themselves as landowners and claimed the native people as their property along with the land.

The new Spanish bureaucracy established a system known as *encomiendas*—estates owned by Spaniards called *encomenderos,* who relied on the indigenous people for labor to mine for precious metals or to grow crops. In theory, the encomenderos were responsible for the lives and health of their subjects. In practice, the only service provided by many encomenderos was conversion to Christianity. Encomenderos may have believed they were saving souls, but converting the slaves did little to prevent hundreds of thousands of deaths.

Priests like the Dominican Bartolomé de las Casas made Spanish royalty aware of the situation, and new royal decrees gave some protection to Native Americans. Indigenous peoples were given back certain (limited) rights, and the encomiendas were slowly dismantled, returning the land to other forms of ownership.

The new laws said nothing about slavery in general, so plantations switched to a labor force imported from Africa. These slaves arrived in the Americas via the *Triangular Trade*, a continuous cycle of shipping that many major

850: Gunpowder is invented in China sometime in the 9th century.

1200: Aztecs begin to purchase cacao from Mayan growers and traders.

1206: Genghis Khan becomes ruler of the Mongols and begins expanding their territory into an empire that will eventually cover most of Eurasia.

1325: The seat of the Aztec empire is established at Tenochtitlan (now Mexico City). *In the next few decades, the largest outbreak of Bubonic Plague in recorded history will begin in Asia and sweep across Europe.*

European countries took part in. On the first leg of the triangle, ships took manufactured goods from Europe to exchange for slaves in Africa. The second leg brought slaves—packed into cargo holds with no regard for their health or safety—across the Pacific to work in mines and on plantations. On the return trip, they carried cash crops like cacao, sugar, tobacco, and cotton back to Europe.

Portugal's Jesuit missionaries were Spain's major rivals in the cacao trade. The Jesuits ran the cacao trade in Brazil, but relied on local labor for the heavy lifting. Missionaries sent indigenous people to collect cacao that already grew wild in the Amazonian rainforest, in addition to enslaving or employing them on plantations.

We did not find sources that centered on the native actions and perspective related to these horrors.

AFRICA: FROM CADBURY TO CHILD SLAVERY

In the late 1700s, Brazil grew around ten percent of the world's cacao and maintained high production levels into the 1820s, when it won independence from Portugal. After Brazil won its independence,

In some legends, the god Quetzalcoatl is credited with bringing cacao to Mesoamerica.

Portugal stayed in the cacao trade by transplanting seedlings to São Tomé, off the western coast of Africa, and then to other equatorial African colonies. Plantation owners offered Africans "jobs" that often turned out to be indentured servitude or slavery.

South America had Bartolomé de las Casas, a respected priest with the ear of the crown who spoke out against slavery and feudalism. Africa had the Religious Society of Friends, commonly known as the Quakers. Quakers had been historically persecuted for their egalitarian religious beliefs and were barred from many professions, but they were often successful in business and well respected for honest practices and quality goods.

⭐ ⭐ ⭐ ⭐ ⭐

CHOCOLATE GOES TO EUROPE

1440: *Johannes Gutenberg invents the printing press.*

1502: Columbus mistakes cacao beans for almonds. Later on the same voyage, he and his crew spend a year stranded on Jamaica.

CACAO SEEDS

1520: Hernán Cortés takes control of Tenochtitlan, seat of the Aztec empire, with the assistance of several other cities in the region. He controls the empire by taking emperor Moctezuma hostage and eventually killing him. Cortés and his soldiers are among the first Europeans to taste chocolate.

1527: Cortés brings cacao beans back to Carlos I of Spain.

1542: Dominican friar Bartolomé de las Casas writes an account of the mistreatment of indigenous people in Spain's American colonies.

1560: Dutch sailors take Criollo cacao trees from Venezuela to Celebes (now Sulawesi, Indonesia).

1582: *While Jesuit missionaries exploit the indigenous people of Brazil as laborers in the cacao industry, another Jesuit, Matteo Ricci, travels the other direction to begin the most substantial direct cultural exchange to date between Europe and China.*

English Quakers brought their concern for fairness and welfare to the chocolate industry with four major family-owned businesses: Fry, Cadbury, Rowntree, and Terry. They shared with the Aztecs a dislike of drunkenness, and thought that chocolate beverages could be a good replacement for alcohol. They also established the predecessor to today's fair trade movement by buying only beans that had been grown without slave labor. Cadbury's radical ideas about labor extended to their workers at home in England as well. They even constructed a utopian factory town in the countryside to get their employees out of urban slums.

Cadbury's original ideals didn't always prevail. In the early 1900s they were purchasing nearly half of their beans from São Tomé, where slavery was commonplace on plantations. Even after this violation was brought to light, Cadbury argued that they could do more for slaves by working with slave-holding Portuguese planters than by finding a different source. But with up to six thousand slaves dying on São Tomé each year the public outcry continued and Quaker chocolatiers returned—at least for a while—to their boycott of slave-grown cacao.

1585: The first major shipment of cacao is sent from Veracruz to Spain.

1600: *While Spain establishes the transatlantic cacao trade, Elizabeth I grants the British East India Company's charter, spurring both English trade with and colonization of India.*

1606: A Florentine merchant brings chocolate to Italy.

1615: A Spanish princess (confusingly named "Anne of Austria") brings cacao to Paris when she is sent to marry Louis XIII. French royalty rapidly establish a tradition of morning cocoa.

1659: David Challiou is named the official chocolatier of Paris.

1697: In London, White's on St. James's Street opens. It caters to high-class clientele who purchase opera tickets while enjoying their cocoa.

1750s: Most Western European nations have cacao plantations in their respective colonies.

1822: The first cacao trees are transplanted to Africa, establishing what will become the world's largest center of cacao production.

With much of the industry boycotting São Tomé, the island's growers shifted away from cacao production. Smaller farms in Ghana and the Ivory Coast, owned and operated by West African families, stepped in to take up the slack. For several decades, they made good money, first under colonial governments and then, for a time, under their own rule. It didn't last.

In the 1950s, farmers in West Africa still found cacao to be a valuable cash crop, but as France and England let go of these former colonies they withdrew financial investment. Ghana and the Ivory Coast started to rely on chocolate farming to support their government and economy. Today, farmers are heavily taxed and must operate through resellers—sometimes several layers of them—to bring their crops to market. Each intermediary takes their cut, as does the government, and industrial chocolate companies in Europe and America are always happy to drive down costs and increase their profit margin.

Between post-colonial disinvestment, class tension, and religious disputes, the economic and political climate in West Africa hasn't been good for cacao growers. Many of them now live in poverty or have turned to other professions. Others make up the gap in a different way: with unpaid child labor. An oft-quoted U.S. State Department report describes conditions on some farms as "the worst forms of child labor." Reporters interviewing plantation workers find a range of stories—from those who were paid and treated well to those who were abducted, purchased from their families, or promised pay and then enslaved. These children endure labor that is almost literally back-breaking, carry heavy loads, and are unlikely to receive any education.

FROM LIQUID TO SOLID: CHOCOLATE INNOVATION

The first solid chocolate in Europe was made around 1674. For over a century prior, Europeans knew only chocolate beverages similar to the ones historically enjoyed by Mesoamericans. Even the solid chocolate of

1674 was coarse and unappetizing, and chocolate bars as we know them today weren't invented until nearly two centuries later.

The story of industrial chocolate began when Fry and Sons replaced water-driven mills with steam engines in the 1700s, around the time of the U.S. Revolutionary War and the French Revolution.

Casparus van Houten patented a new technique for processing cacao in 1828, using hydraulic press. His son, Coenraad, later developed the alkalizing or "dutching" process that makes cocoa powder sweeter and helps it dissolve in water. (page 25)

In 1847, the same year that Charlotte Brontë published *Jane Eyre*, Francis Fry created an "eating chocolate" by adding cocoa butter back into van Houten's cocoa powder. It was much grainier than what we eat today, but still more palatable than the early versions. Cadbury followed with their own eating chocolate two years later.

The British Quaker companies may have created the first chocolate bars, but Swiss inventors made some crucial

BEFORE FAIR TRADE: SÃO TOMÉ AND THE QUAKERS

The Quaker chocolatiers of England promoted chocolate, tea, and coffee as alternatives to alcohol. Like their peers in the United States, they were known for championing abolition and labor rights. The major Quaker chocolate companies found it difficult to stick to their morals, however, in the slave-fueled cacao trade.

1791-1804: Haitian plantation slaves rebel. This Haitian Revolution leads to independence, though Haiti is economically devastated by extreme French reparation demands a couple decades later.

1820: The first cacao trees are transplanted to São Tomé, off Africa's west coast.

1824: John Cadbury, a Quaker, begins selling tea, coffee, and chocolate.

1840: Māori Chiefs sign the Treaty of Waitangi, written by British representatives, setting New Zealand up for centuries of disputed governance and ownership.

1866: J. S. Fry & Sons, another Quaker company, begins producing their Chocolate Cream bar over a century after Joseph

Fry's first chocolate-making experiments.

1876: Portugal abolishes slavery, but maintains an extreme form of indentured servitude on São Tomé and Príncipe because it is the only way to keep chocolate plantations profitable.

1893: John Cadbury's son, George, buys land for a company town to improve living conditions for his employees.

1905: Cadbury introduces the Dairy Milk bar, which rapidly becomes their top product.

1906: Journalist Henry Nevinson publishes a book detailing slave labor in São Tomé and Príncipe.

1909: After years of public pressure, Cadbury, Fox, and Rowntree begin to boycott São Tomé.

1913: São Tomé's chocolate production peaks at 36,500 tons per year.

1973: Without Cadbury and other major customers, São Tomé is producing only 12,000 tons of chocolate per year when it becomes independent of Portugal.

2005: With Portuguese investment gone, São Tomé produces only 3,000 tons of chocolate each year.

improvements. Daniel Peter added Henri Nestlé's powdered milk to create milk chocolate, and the two went into business together under Nestlé's name. Rudolph Lindt developed the conching machine, which mixes and melts chocolate for up to 72 hours to smooth it.

In 1861, Cadbury began to sell heart-shaped chocolate boxes for Valentine's Day, and in 1895 the big name in American chocolate entered the scene when Milton S. Hershey sold his first chocolate bar.

CHOCOLATE AS WE KNOW IT

At the beginning of the twentieth century, the cost of sugar and cacao suddenly dropped, making chocolate bars affordable to the masses in a way they hadn't been before. Between economic shifts, more efficient manufacturing, and new marketing techniques, chocolate really became the product we know today.

Forrest Gump famously said, "Life is like a box of chocolates." That box of chocolates as we know it was invented by Louise Agostini. Her husband, Jean Neuhaus, created the first Belgian pralines. Neuhaus was a pharmacist who coated medicine

with chocolate to make it more palatable, but in 1912, he began to experiment with powdered milk and other candy fillings. Within a year, a Swiss chocolatier mechanized the process and sold a box of chocolates, and in 1920, Agostini designed the "ballotin"—the molded plastic inset that her husband, and many other chocolatiers, used to keep chocolates from sliding around in their boxes.

Agostini and Neuhaus's *ballotins* were beautiful displays of chocolate, perfect for gifting, but they weren't the only Belgians to try innovative marketing. A company called Leonidas decided to bring chocolate to the masses at a reasonable price and with minimal packaging by selling it from an open counter on the street: a walk-up chocolate bar.

While the Belgians and Swiss made the proverbial box of chocolates, others developed their own machinery for mass production. Industrialization took its toll, though. In 1915, Heinrich Stollwerck, one of five German brothers to develop early machinery for mass-producing chocolate bars, drowned in his own chocolate when a machine exploded.

Marketing and mechanization weren't the only realms of innovation for the cacao industry. In 1925, the New York Cocoa Exchange was established for trading cocoa futures. For people in the cacao industry, the Exchange offered an opportunity to hedge their bets against future price fluctuations. Unfortunately, it also gave speculators an opportunity to play the market, and if speculative trades aren't sufficiently regulated they can harm both growers and buyers of cacao.

CHOCOLATE AT WAR

In 1825, the Royal Navy consumed more hot chocolate than all the rest of Britain combined. They served it to sailors on watch duty because it was warm, invigorating, and non-alcoholic. They were neither the first nor the last military force to see value in chocolate. Many ancient Mesoamerican societies treated cocoa as an energy drink for soldiers and messengers, and the tradition has continued into the modern day.

Soldiers in both world wars were provided with chocolate as part of their field rations, though it was meant only for emergencies. To prevent soldiers from indulging, their chocolate bars were formulated to taste "a little better than a boiled potato," according to the Hershey Archives. In the United Kingdom after World War II, when chocolate rationing ended for the general public, so many people rushed to buy chocolate that rationing was reinstated for another four years while production caught up with demand.

When the Soviet Union blockaded West Berlin, the American and British governments coordinated an airlift of food and other supplies that involved over 1,500 flights per day at its peak. While the operation wouldn't have been possible without precise coordination, its success in the public mind was largely thanks to pilot Gail Halvorsen, who dropped chocolate bars from his plane to the children of West Berlin. The "candy bomber," with his parachutes made from handkerchiefs and his concern for the happiness of children, secured the operation's public image.

FAIR TRADE: THE MARKET-DRIVEN ANSWER

Legislation in Europe and the U.S. that would have placed an embargo on slave-made chocolate has largely failed. It has fallen to advocates and concerned members of the industry to develop piecemeal certification programs and best practices for ethical trade. The best-known of these is *fair trade* labeling, a group of certification programs that require buyers of cacao to pay growers an above-market rate and certify farmers based on their labor practices. The standards for fair trade labeling are set by a handful of major fair trade networks.

Labeling and certification initiatives like fair trade have been criticized for a variety of reasons. They tend to be focused on marketing, providing a marginal increase in price for growers without giving them a real route out of poverty. According to *Fair Trade, Corporate Accountability, and Beyond*, fair trade farmers see about eight cents of each dollar spent on chocolate. The remaining 92% goes to bulk buyers, shippers, commodity brokers, chocolatiers,

taxes, and—in the case of fair trade and Organic products—to the certifying organizations. Perhaps the ultimate issue is that fair trade certifiers are trying to solve problems with the same market-based tools that caused them in the first place.

SOME BETTER SOLUTIONS: LOCAL OWNERSHIP AND DIRECT TRADE

Fair trade programs might increase a grower's profit margin by a few percent, but it will take a radical change in trade dynamics to shift the balance of economic inequity. Divine Chocolate represents one model for this change— the growers' cooperative that supplies cacao for Divine bars also owns a majority 44% share in Divine. They have ownership over the entire supply chain, and reap the same benefits as any other shareholders.

Direct trade is another alternative to fair trade certification. Like fair trade, it is a term used by chocolatiers to describe their bean-buying practices. Rather than operating within the conventional chocolate supply chain and paying a premium for certification, direct trade chocolate companies establish relationships

DIEGO'S CHOCOLATE: PRODUCED WHERE IT'S GROWN

There's a place in Guatemala with a beautiful view of Lake Atitlan where a Mayan man named Diego makes chocolate with his family. Starting from his grandmother's recipe, he experimented until he had created a solid bar worth selling to the tourists nearby. The result is unique in several ways.

Farmers from nearby Costa Sur (a major cacao growing region since the pre-Classic Maya period) bring their beans right to Diego in the most direct of direct trades. Without brokers or shippers to pay, Diego can pay farmers a price that beats fair trade premiums without breaking the bank.

The beans are processed less than they would be in a recipe from the European tradition—ground once, rather than continuously conched over several days. Diego sweetens the chocolate with *panela*, unrefined cane sugar that he buys from small Central American producers. The minimally refined ingredients make for a grainier chocolate than we're accustomed

to, but it melts in your mouth like nothing else.

The chocolate is sold in cigar-shaped rolls, wrapped with wax paper and then brightly colored tissue paper. The pretty labels, showing that beautiful view of Lake Atitlan, are each colored by hand. Diego could have them printed, but he would rather employ someone locally for the job.

with individual growers. Direct trade chocolatiers often visit plantations to evaluate growing and working conditions while cultivating partnerships with individual farmers. Most of these are small "bean-to-bar" companies that do everything from roasting to conching molding to sales in-house. Direct trade isn't governed by a certifying body, so various companies interpret the term differently, but many have established codes of ethics that guide their buying practices.

Diego's Chocolate in Guatemala and Madécasse in Madagascar offer a radical answer to concerns about trade dynamics and global economic inequality. By growing, producing, and packaging chocolate locally in their respective countries, they retain most of the profit that would otherwise go to chocolatiers in the global north.

Ultimately, fair trade and direct trade are incomplete solutions. Poverty and lack of education prevent many growers from producing better quality crops, driving a harder bargain with buyers, or moving into higher-profit segments of the chocolate supply chain. There is no single solution, but right now it seems like the easiest thing we can do as consumers is buy chocolate made in ways that allow everyone in the chocolate industry to have a good quality of life and build healthy communities.

We want to thank the many authors and researchers whose work forms the basis of this book. There is a more extensive bibliography at the end of the book, but here is a short list of recommendations for anyone who wants to learn more about chocolate:

The True History of Chocolate by Sophie D. Coe and Michael D. Coe—If I had to take a single book about chocolate with me to a desert island, this would be my choice. It's full of fascinating information and fantastic tales

about chocolate's history and production, woven together in a narrative so engaging I had a hard time remembering to stop and take notes. It also has an extensive bibliography.

Chocolate: A Bittersweet Saga of Dark and Light by **Mort Rosenblum**— This book is just plain (informative) fun. Rosenblum is an experienced journalist, and it shows in this engaging, well-crafted story of his travels around the world to explore different aspects of chocolate production and consumption.

The Candy Bombers: The Untold Story of the Berlin Airlift and America's Finest Hour by **Andrei Cherny**—We only had room for a few paragraphs about the Berlin Airlift and Gail Halvorsen's ingenious candy-drops to the children of Berlin, but Andrei Cherny spends over six hundred pages on the logistics of the airlift and the role Halvorsen played in publicizing and popularizing it.

Chocolate as Medicine: A Quest over the Centuries by **Philip K. Wilson and W. Jeffery Hurst**—People have been claiming that chocolate is good (or, sometimes, bad) since the beginning of its recorded history. The truth of the matter is, at best, difficult to get at and still uncertain, but Wilson and Hurst offer a good preliminary overview for anyone who is interested—plus a wealth of odd tales both ancient and modern about all the different medicinal properties attributed to chocolate. For up-to-the-minute information, though, your best bet is to trawl scientific and medical journals in search of meta-studies and literature reviews. Popular medical reporting can lead you to potentially interesting stories, but be sure to follow up and read the referenced papers whenever possible!

∾CHOCOLATE DISAMBIGUATION∾

*C*hocolate comes in many forms and goes by many names. Words like cocoa have context-dependent and regionally variable meanings. It all gets a bit confusing at times (even for us) so here's a quick guide to the terminology.

COCOA AND CACAO

"Cacao" probably comes from the word *kakawa* in languages of the Mixe-Zoquean family, which include that spoken by the Olmec people. Mixe-Zoquean languages date back to at least 1000 BC, but they are still spoken in parts of Mexico. Later Mesoamerican languages borrowed words from Mixe-Zoquean, and kakawa was one of them. The Mayans took it directly, while the Aztecs altered it to *cacahuatl.*

Spanish colonists, however, didn't pick up kakawa/cacahuatl—possibly because in Spanish *caca* means "shit." Instead they adapted chocolate from *xocolatl,* an Aztec word that referred to chocolate beverages, though its literal translation is "bitter water."

CACAO: *Theobroma Cacao* is the scientific name for the tree that produces chocolate. Cacao is sometimes used when referring to raw or minimally processed products, like cacao beans. It is also used interchangeably with cocoa.

The Mayan symbol for Kakawa

COCOA: This is sometimes shorthand for "hot cocoa." Otherwise, it is used along with cacao to describe a wide range of chocolate products.

BEANS AND NIBS

When Christopher Columbus and his crew first saw cacao beans, they called them almonds. It is an understandable mistake, because the beans are similar in size, shape, and color. Cacao beans are a bit less wrinkly, and they are rounded at both ends instead of teardrop shaped. Once they are fermented and dried, the fibrous shell comes off easily and the inner part of the bean can be cracked into smaller chunks, known as *nibs*.

You can buy cacao beans and nibs in natural grocery stores, often in bulk. With the recent popularity of raw foods it's not unusual to see bagged nibs in the "health food" section of large chains as well.

COCOA LIQUOR

This is a common industry term, but it's not sold to consumers under that name. Cocoa liquor is the paste you get from grinding up cacao beans. It does not contain alcohol, and is called "liquor" because it is liquid when warm.

BAKING WITH COCOA POWDER

Alkalization—or lack thereof—is important when you are baking with chemical leaveners. Baking soda relies on an external source of acid to produce the carbon dioxide bubbles that make baked goods rise. In many chocolate recipes, un-alkalized cocoa powder provides that acidity, and switching to the alkalized variety will leave you with a flat cake. Similarly, a brownie recipe that calls for alkalized cocoa is more likely to use baking powder, which brings its own acid. Un-alkalized cocoa can add too much acidity and change the balance of the reaction. While we only use un-alkalized cocoa for recipes in this book, many recipes don't specify the type, so you have to guess based on other ingredients. Baking powder or acids like lemon juice and buttermilk in an ingredient list are all good indications that the author's cocoa powder was alkalized.

COCOA POWDER

If you take cocoa liquor and squeeze out most of the fat, you'll have a "press cake"—a solid block of cocoa solids. Grind it up and you get cocoa powder, a dry form of chocolate that is often more convenient to cook with than bars or nibs.

DUTCHING OR ALKALIZING

Chocolate is fairly acidic. Many manufacturers add an alkaline substance like potassium carbonate to the nibs, liquor, or powder to balance that acidity. This process is sometimes called "dutching" because it was invented in the 1800s by Dutch chocolatier Coenraad Johannes van Houten, son of the man who made the first press cake using a hydraulic press.

Chocolate for bars and confections is usually un-alkalized, but cocoa powder is often dutched to make it darker and milder. Dutching may also allow cocoa powder to dissolve more easily when making beverages. Alkalizing may have some negative impact on the flavonoid content of cacao, so look for un-alkalized if heart health is your interest—see the Science chapter (page 172) for details.

COCOA BUTTER

When you press the fat out of chocolate to make cocoa powder, the result is cocoa butter—a plant oil that has been in high demand recently, especially for cosmetics. Cocoa butter is solid at room temperature and slightly harder than coconut oil. It has a deceptively alluring chocolate scent, but the flavor is very subtle. The first time I encountered it I was so amazed by the scent that I took a small bite, only to discover that it tastes like a mouthful of vegetable shortening.

Some chocolate bars replace most of the cocoa butter with cheaper fats like palm oil. In bars with very low cacao contents, the difference can be hard to notice, but it changes the consistency of the chocolate.

We store our cocoa butter in a mason jar. To get liquid out of the jar, we put a pan of water on the stove and put the jar in the pan of water until there is enough usable liquid. We always remove the lid on the off-chance that leaving the lid on would pressurize the jar to the point of explosion. It's possible that this repeated double boiling process has reduced the lifespan of our cocoa butter, but it has worked well for us, and we find this method preferable to losing any unscrape-able cocoa butter to the sides of a double boiler. If the fact that it's solid at room temperature is going to be a problem, you can cut it fifty-fifty with a vegetable oil that's liquid at room temperature.

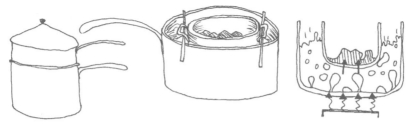

A COUPLE OF SIMPLE DOUBLE BOILERS.

HARD CHOCOLATE: BARS AND BAKING CHOCOLATE

Until around the end of the 20th century, chocolate makers in the United States were very secretive about their recipes. Information like the cocoa content of a bar or the origin of the beans was considered a trade secret. Within a few decades, it has become commonplace to share all sorts of details—a good thing for cooking with chocolate, because it helps us know what we're getting when we buy a bar.

Every time I check, it's cheaper at our most-frequented grocery stores to buy a fair trade dark chocolate bar from the chocolate section than to buy the same thing in different packaging in the baking aisle. The sugar in the chocolate bar is just the right amount to pre-balance the bitterness of the cocoa, and it's not as drying as powder, so this is usually our go-to for hot entrees.

NAMES AND PERCENTAGES

Unsweetened chocolate, including some baking chocolate, is effectively a bar of solidified cocoa liquor. It's extremely bitter and most often used with sweeteners when cooking or baking. It may also be labeled as 99% or 100% chocolate.

Semisweet and bittersweet or dark and extra-dark chocolate have some sugar added, and are often interchangeable for baking. In the United States, both are required to have at least 35% cacao, but bittersweet more often refers to percentages over seventy.

Sweet chocolate contains 15–35% cacao and is quite mild.

BEVERAGES

Chocolate goes in so many different kinds of beverages! Name a drink, there's a chocolate version.

BREWED CHOCOLATE

Brewed chocolate is a must-try in the world of cocoa beverages. It's similar to a cup of coffee, except that it tastes like chocolate. If you have access to a grinder that won't blend so fast that it melts your nibs, you can grind your beans to maximize flavor by exposing more surface area during the brewing process, but mincing with a knife works great, too. If you're using cocoa beans, wash them well or remove the papery outer husk. This beverage is simple, easy to make, and a new classic in our household.

Makes 1 mug
Takes 10–20 minutes

1 mug water
2 tablespoons minced cocoa beans or nibs

Put water on to boil. Put the nibs in a tea ball, and steep them in freshly-boiled water for 5–15 minutes. Enjoy!

BREWED CHOCOLATE WITH CARDAMOM: Chop up a pod's worth of cardamom and steep it along with the cocoa beans.

CHOCOLATE SMOOTHIE

We love this recipe for its simplicity and reliable tastiness. Stick to the more intense fruits for flavor, and use bland fruits such as apples, bananas, and pears for substance and sweetness. Avoid using citrus; it's too pulpy. If the fruit doesn't come out sweet enough on its own, substitute 1/4 cup of chocolate chips for the cocoa powder. Now is the time to use up any ugly, abandoned, or forgotten fruit; it still tastes delicious in a smoothie!

Makes about 2 cups
Takes about 10 minutes

10 ounces frozen local fruits (blueberries, strawberries, mango, etc.)
3 tablespoons cocoa powder and/or 1/4 cup chocolate chips
Plant milk (as needed)
2 tablespoons nut butter or seeds (optional)
Spices (optional)

Drop the fruit into the blender, and add the cocoa powder. If you're using chocolate chips, don't add them yet. Add any nut butter and spices. Pour in enough plant milk into the blender to just cover the berries.

Blend until smooth, which is usually when you start to see a consistent funnel shape swirling at the top of the smoothie. Depending on the blender, you may need to turn it off briefly and use a utensil to jab at the fruit a little to break it up, or add a little more plant milk to help it blend.

After the smoothie is smooth, drop the chocolate chips into the blender and blend them until they reach the size you'd prefer. They turn into micro-chips very quickly, so this may only take a few seconds.

Use a rubber spatula to scrape every last drop of smoothie from the blender into a glass.

COCOA MASALA CHAI

Karha Masala, or chai, is a blend of tea and other spices. There is so much variation in chai spices. We use several variations on karha masala that work well with cocoa. Here's one simple recipe that uses ingredients you may already have on hand. Plain black tea is the most commonly used tea, but you can also use Earl Grey (the bergamot in Earl Grey is a citrus oil, and citrus goes well both with chocolate and in chai) or even green tea or rooibos.

When heating your water, with black tea you're looking for the "rope of pearls" stage; about 200°F. Otherwise, "just below boiling" should work fine! For green teas, heat the water as hot as 180°F (any bubbles up to the size of fish eyes, or boil and wait a couple minutes) may be appropriate. For rooibos, go all out and aim for the rolling boil of a forgotten tea kettle. Hot chocolate is even easier! It doesn't require a specific water temperature.

1 tablespoon cocoa powder
1 teaspoon tea leaves
1/4 teaspoon powdered allspice
1/4 teaspoon powdered star anise
1/4 teaspoon powdered black pepper
1/4 teaspoon powdered cardamom
1/4 teaspoon powdered cinnamon
1/4 teaspoon powdered cloves
1/4 teaspoon powdered ginger
Soy milk (optional)
Sweetener (optional)

Heat water in a kettle or saucepan.

Meanwhile, put your tea in a tea ball and drop it into a mug. In the same mug, combine the cocoa powder, allspice, anise, pepper, cardamom, cinnamon, cloves, and ginger.

When the water has reached your desired temperature, add enough to fill the bottom quarter of the mug and stir it into the cocoa powder and spices. Add more water and steep for three to five minutes.

Remove the tea ball and add soy milk and sweetener if you want them.

SIMPLE METHOD: For a simple cocoa chai, add cocoa to a plain tea or premixed chai. Either way, it's taste-tea!

CHAMPURRADO

Champurrado is a creamy hot chocolate that is thickened with corn flour, and traditionally sold with tamales as a breakfast-on-the-go by *tamaleros* in the streets of Mexican cities. Even if you don't have a tamalero handy, champurrado is not to be missed! It can be spiced with cinnamon, anise, or vanilla. Muchas gracias to our fine illustrator, Cat Callaway, for helping us figure out the right search terms to learn about champurrado.

Makes one cupful
Takes 15 minutes

Fry up some churros. They're simple to make, and are served side by side with champurrado.

MOLINILLO
FOR FROTHING
CHOCOLATE,
NORMALLY MADE
OF WOOD

8 ounces plant milk
2 tablespoons cocoa powder
1 1/2 tablespoons sugar
2 tablespoons corn flour (masa harina)

Simmer the plant milk, cocoa powder, and sugar over medium heat, stirring, until the sugar and cocoa are completely mixed in. Add the corn flour and continue to stir for about 10 minutes, making sure no corn flour sticks to the bottom of the pot. Serve warm.

Some traditional recipes call for champurrado to be frothed with a *molinillo*, the traditional Mexican chocolate whisk. If you want a a lighter beverage but don't have a molinillo of your own, an immersion blender will do the trick.

★ ★ ★ ★ ★   11   ★ ★ ★ ★ ★

CHERRY CHOCOLATE MILK

If at all possible, this beautiful pink beverage should be served in a clear glass.

Makes one pint
Takes 30 minutes

1 red beet (for beet water)
2 cups of plant milk
5 teaspoons cocoa powder
5 teaspoons cherry jam or other sweetener
1/2 teaspoon cherry flavoring

Cube the beet for another recipe, such as "Hummus of the Gods" (page 88). Boil the beet for the boiled beet water. When the beet is cooked, reserve 2 tablespoons of the beet water for immediate use, and pour the rest off into an ice cube tray for coloring future cherry chocolate milk or turning pretty much everything you cook red for a while.

Simmer the milk on low heat in a small pot, stirring, until you start to see steam rising from the surface. Remove the milk from the heat and add the cocoa powder, jam, beet water, and cherry flavoring. Whisk until everything except the cherry from the jam is well-dissolved. To enjoy the delights of delayed gratification, put your cherry chocolate milk in the fridge, wait, and drink it cold.

FAST & SIMPLE CHERRY CHOCOLATE MILK The full recipe gives a more nuanced blend of flavors, but here's the five-minute version. In a pint glass, combine 2 tablespoons of chocolate syrup, 1 cup plant milk, and 1/2 teaspoon cherry flavoring. Drop in a few shreds of fresh red beet if you have a beet handy and stir everything well with a dessert spoon. Stir in the remaining cup of plant milk and serve.

FRESH CHERRY CHOCOLATE MILK *What?!* Cherries are in season! Forget about that beet! Bust out the red cherries! Blend together a glass of plant milk, a handful of pitted red cherries, and 4 teaspoons of cocoa powder. Serve in a glass with a dessert spoon.

DRINKING CHOCOLATE

We used to work at a shop that offered bike tours of our city, and one of their stops was at a chocolate shop called "Cacao" that offers flights of three different shots of the richest drinking chocolate ever. We loved their drinking chocolate so much, we learned to make it at home. Here's our plant-based version:

Fills 3–4 espresso cups
Takes 15 minutes

1/2 cup coconut milk
1/2 cup soy milk
3 ounce dark chocolate bar

Chop up the chocolate bar. Pour the coconut milk and soy milk into a small pot and mix it all up with a fork until you've de-lumped the coconut fat.

Heat the combined milks on low, stirring frequently. Keep a close eye on them, and when the first sign of steam shows up, immediately reduce the temperature to low. Stir in the chocolate until it's melted. Serve immediately in espresso cups.

BICERIN: An Italian layered beverage so intensely rich that its very name means "small glass." In a small glass, pour a shot of espresso. Add the drinking chocolate and top it all off with an aquafaba-based whipped cream.

MINI FUDGESICLES: Distribute leftovers evenly in an ice cube tray and store them in the freezer. If you want to be all fancy about serving them, put 1–2 cubes on a small plate, top with a little raspberry sauce and garnish with mint. We just eat these straight from the freezer any time we open up the freezer to look for something.

HOT CHOCOLATE

When it's wet, grey, and cold outside, curling up with a cup of hot cocoa can be the most comforting experience.

Makes one cupful
Takes 5 minutes

3 tablespoons cocoa powder
2 tablespoons sugar
1 teaspoon vanilla extract

Put some water on to boil. While you're waiting, put all the ingredients in the bottom of a mug. When the water is ready, cover the mixture with hot water and mix the ingredients together into a syrup. This helps prevent little pockets of cocoa powder from floating to the surface of your drink. Then fill the mug the rest of the way. Stir and enjoy!

CHOCOLATE IN CHURCH

In 1569, Pope Pius V decreed that cocoa was a beverage, and therefore permissible during Lent. He thought it thoroughly unpleasant, and therefore not a risk of moral harm. Not everyone in the church agreed with him, though.

In the mid-1650s Bishop Don Bernardino de Salazar threatened to excommunicate the ladies of his Mexican congregation because their habit of drinking chocolate in church interrupted his sermons. The ladies switched congregations, and the bishop died soon after—supposedly from a poisoned cup of chocolate.

Here are some well-loved variations on the theme of hot cocoa:

BULK HOT COCOA: Fill a container with a 3:2 ratio of cocoa powder to sugar (or adjust it to taste). That's really all there is to it! A 1/4 cup measure makes a good scoop for transferring it to your glass.

CHOCOLATE ORANGE: Add 1/4 teaspoon orange extract. It's like drinking a chocolate orange.

CON LECHE: Replace water with your preferred plant milk. Heat the milk until steam is just rising off the surface. Continue with the instructions as described above.

FRUIT AT THE BOTTOM: Replace the sugar with 1/4 cup of jam or marmalade. The fruit at the bottom will be somewhat bland, but that's because it gave a little complexity to your hot cocoa. Stir well!

MEXICAN HOT CHOCOLATE: Add ground cinnamon or be extra-fancy and ostentatiously use a grater to grate some cinnamon fresh from the stick.

MINT: Carefully add mint essential oil. We use 10–20 drops. For a more natural flavor, steep mint leaves in the hot cocoa like you would to make mint tea.

MULLED COCOA: Add mulling spices.

RED COCOA: Annatto grows in the same forests as cacao and has been used in Mayan cocoa beverages as far back as 800 AD.

SUBTLE TEA

White tea is an extravagance because it uses only the new leaves and buds of the tea plant. Even so, this tea is just too exquisite not to share. Drink it from your favorite teacup.

Makes 1 (6-ounce) mug
Takes 10–15 minutes

1 teaspoon white tea leaves
1 teaspoon cocoa nibs, minced

Heat the water in a covered pot until it reaches about 180°F, or bubbles the size of crab eyes plus some steam. While the water is heating, put the tea leaves and nibs in a tea ball. Put the tea ball in a mug, pour the hot water into the mug, and steep the tea for three minutes. Remove the tea ball and serve. Share and enjoy!

In most languages, the word "tea" uses te, cha, or chai as its root word. "Etymology of tea" is a great search term if you would like to geek out about language. Now go forth and brew some tea!

THICK CHOCOLATE BANANA DRINK

This drink makes a delicious breakfast treat. It's just like a milkshake, but without the dairy or refined sugar!

Makes one glass
Takes 10 minutes

1 frozen banana
1 cup plant milk
1/4 cup coconut cream
2 tablespoons grated unsweetened baking chocolate
1 teaspoon vanilla extract
1/8 teaspoon cardamom

Break the banana up into a few chunks. Dump all the ingredients into the blender. Blend everything. Pour the drink into a glass and drink it while it's cold.

"THE MANNER OF MAKING CHOCOLATE"

This recipe is from "Chocolate: or, An Indian Drinke" (1631) by Antonio Colmenero de Ledesma, which is an extremely entertaining read, and available on Project Gutenberg. This version was published in English in 1652 by Captain James Wadsworth during the Golden Age of Piracy. Both the book and the chocolate were sold at the Vine Tavern in Holberne.

Set a Pot of Conduit Water over the fire untill it boiles, then to every person that is to drink, put an ounce of Chocolate, with as much Sugar into another Pot; wherein you must poure a pint of the said boiling Water, and therein mingle the Chocolate and the Sugar, with the instrument called El Molinillo, untill it be thoroughly incorporated: which done, poure in as many halfe pints of the said Water as there be ounces of Chocolate, and if you please, you may put in one or two yelks of fresh Eggs, which must be beaten untill they froth very much; the hotter it is drunke, the better it is, being cold it may doe harme. You may likewise put in a slice of white bred or Bisquet, and eate that with the Chocolate. The newer and fresher made it is, the more benefit you shall finde by it; that which comes from forreigne parts, and is stale, is not so good as that which is made here.

1630s SPANISH HOT CHOCOLATE

We translated the preceding recipe for hot chocolate from the 1630s into something you can make at home. The egg yolk is optional even in the original recipe. If you don't have access to yard eggs, we recommend that you omit the yolk—it will still be a tasty plant-based rendition of an antique hot chocolate. You may also wish to omit the yolk if you're very young, very old, have a compromised immune system, or don't eat animal products. In that era, sugar was for the gentry, so this recipe has a lot of sugar. It's very sweet.

Makes about 2 pints
Takes 20 minutes

4 cups clean water
1/4 cup grated baking chocolate
1/4 cup sugar
One fresh egg yolk (optional)
Fresh white bread or biscuits (optional)

First, you'll need access to clean water, which may be a little easier today than it was in 17th century Europe. We initially assumed the "Conduit Water" that the recipe calls for would have come from an aqueduct, but it turns out the term actually refers to spring water! For most of you, clean municipal tap water is an adequate substitute.

Next, boil your water. If it's an option, boil your water in a covered pot over an open fire. If you don't have access to an open fire, any method will do. In a small pot, whisk together the boiling water, grated baking chocolate, and the sugar. Use a molinillo if you have one, otherwise, a common whisk or a fork will do.

41

Are you wondering what they used that leftover egg white for? At the time, sugar came in a large, cone-shaped *sugar loaf*, and once you had broken off some lumps of sugar, you'd still need to clarify the sugar to get the impurities out. We're not entirely clear on the details of the process, but it seemed to involve blood (called *spice*) and/or egg white and/or egg yolk. In any case, it was definitely not vegan. These days, some sugar is refined using bone char, but entirely plant-based refined sugar is also available.

This recipe comes from the preindustrial 1630s, so when it calls for a fresh egg, we mean that if you don't have a hen, find a friend who raises chickens. Then invite yourself over to make them antique hot chocolate, and schedule your date for the time of day when there is usually an egg still hot from the hen. If your egg has been refrigerated, let the yolk sit out at room temperature for a while so it froths easier. Beat the egg yolk until it's very frothy, then add it to the beverage.

Pour the cocoa into a couple of mugs. Serve frothy and very hot with bread or biscuits.

BONUS BEVERAGES

A basic chocolate drink: Cocoa powder + spice + water/plant milk is a formula that will take you far. Serve hot or cold.

Caffè mocha: A friend of mine once had a dog named Mocha. Mocha was a wonderful dog, and this is a tasty beverage. You can think of it as a latte plus chocolate, or as a hot chocolate plus espresso. Make a mocha.

Cocoa chicha: There are lots of different kinds of chicha, but it is usually a corn beer. Cocoa corn beer: give it a go.

Kombucha: If you like making kombucha, experiment with steeping minced cocoa nibs and other herbs and spices in with the kombucha for a day or so before straining them out. Most people who make kombucha have some SCOBY they'd love to give away if you ask around.

Tejate: According to Cat Callaway, our illustrator, "TEJATE IS DELICIOUS"! Furthermore, she says that "tejate is a drink that apparently only exists in Oaxaca City and its surroundings. Not coastal Oaxaca, not in the Oaxacan Sierra, just in the valley where Oaxaca City is situated. This is what I've been told by some Oaxacans." We had no luck finding some of the ingredients, so keep an eye out for this non-alcoholic beverage if you're ever in Oaxaca City!

FROTHING TEJATE

Wine: Serve chocolate with a dessert wine, flavor wine with cocoa, or make wine from cocoa pulp.

DESSERTS

AQUAFABA CASHEW GANACHE **BY GOOSE WOHLT**

Chocolate ganache is typically made from chocolate and cream. In this recipe, the combination of blended cashews and aquafaba with a touch of coconut oil act as the cream substitute.

This recipe can be a bit temperamental to match up with the variation in aquafaba consistencies available, but once you find the right balance of aquafaba, cashew, and chocolate, it makes a super easy and quick dark-chocolate ganache. Using cashew cream made from aquafaba resulted in a nice and glossy ganache, even when set, without imparting any discernible bean or cashew flavor. The best part? It only takes a few minutes to whip together.

If you don't have 2/3 cup of aquafaba, top it off with water. Between the aquafaba and cashews, there is enough emulsification to prevent it from seizing the chocolate. The amount of cashews, aquafaba, and chocolate will determine how thick the final ganache is. If your aquafaba is really thick, use fewer cashews. If it's really watery, go with the higher amount.

Makes 2–3 cups
Takes 15 minutes

8 ounces 50–70% dark chocolate
1/2–3/4 cup raw cashews, as needed
3/4 cup aquafaba
1 tablespoon refined coconut oil
1/2 teaspoon vanilla extract
1/8 teaspoon salt

Put the chocolate in a medium-sized bowl and set it aside, along with a lid that will cover it, for when you're done blending the other ingredients.

In a vitamix or other high speed blender, combine cashews, aquafaba, coconut oil, vanilla, and salt.

Blend on highest speed for no more than 3 minutes. The idea is to get the cashews as creamy as possible and steaming hot, but not so hot that they cook and emulsify. If your mixture doesn't pour out of the blender without scraping when you're done, it probably got too hot or there are too many cashews for your aquafaba. It should be like thick cream, not pudding. I don't need to scrape the blender.

If you don't have a high speed blender, you need to soak the cashews in water overnight before blending. If you don't have time to soak the nuts, you can microwave or boil them for 5 minutes and leave to sink in the hot water for 20 minutes. A high speed blender like a Vitamix will heat it up on its own in short order, so you don't need the additional soaking or heating steps.[1]

Once the cashew cream is hot, pour it over the chocolate and cover the bowl. Let the bowl sit, undisturbed, for four minutes, but not too much longer because you don't want it to cool down too much. Stir it all together quickly until completely uniform. You want the chocolate

---

1 *We found that our small "Magic Bullet" blender heated the mixture to steaming, but your blender may vary.*

to melt slowly, but not get too cold. Stir it until there are no more chocolate lumps.

Final temperature should be right at 88–89° F (31° C).

If you're using it to pour onto something, you can pour right away. Or, cool it in the fridge for a bit to harden and roll into balls for dipping in tempered chocolate.

CHOCOLATE FROSTING: Eight ounces of chocolate will give you a fudge-like consistency when it sets up. If you want something closer to a wet frosting, go with less chocolate (e.g., 6 ounces).

While we were writing this cookbook, we learned about this new-fangled ingredient called *aquafaba*. "Aqua" as in water, and "faba" as in bean. You may know it as the viscous water that garbanzo beans are packed in. Turns out that viscousness means it can do all sorts of amazing tricks! Plant-based meringue, anyone? Seriously. Aquafaba. It's blowing minds and rocking the vegan world.

Goose Wohlt coined the name "aquafaba" and was the first to use it to make a vegan meringue in 2015. Shortly thereafter, Rebecca August started the "hits & misses" Facebook group where all the initial aquafaba experimentation emerged. These two luminaries of the aquafaba community have both graciously agreed to include a recipe for this cookbook. Serendipitously, their two recipes complement each other perfectly.

CHOCOLATE MIDNIGHT CAKE

My recipe is based on the famous vegan "wacky cake," as modified by a friend of mine, Sunday Harvie. I reduced the sugar by a 1/4 cup, and subbed half the oil with aquafaba. It is very moist and holds together well, with a lovely crumb. Aquafaba gives cakes a certain bounce that is very appealing.[1]

[1] *Frost this cake with 1 1/2–2 cups of Goose's Aquafaba Cashew Chocolate Frosting (page 50).*

Makes one 9 x 12-inch cake or two 6-inch rounds
Takes 60 minutes

2 cups flour
1 cup sugar
1/2 cup unsweetened cocoa powder
1 tablespoon baking soda
1/2 teaspoon salt
1 cup unsweetened soymilk or other plant milk
1/3 cup safflower, canola or sunflower oil
1/3 cup aquafaba, in liquid form (not whipped)
1 cup strong hot coffee

Preheat oven to 350°F.

Combine flour, sugar, cocoa, baking soda, and salt; add soymilk and oil and aquafaba, and blend with a spoon. Stir in hot coffee. The batter will be very thin, but don't worry!

Pour into two 6" round pans lined with parchment paper, or 9 by 12-inch pan. Bake at 350°F for about 40 minutes (your time may vary, so please start checking around the 30 minute mark, since my oven temp is unreliable). Keep checking frequently until the center is set and a toothpick comes out clean. Don't overbake!

Cool and frost.

BANANANANA BREAD

"Nanny Ogg knew how to start spelling 'banana', but didn't know how you stopped." -Terry Pratchett

I love fresh yellow bananas as a special treat. When they start to go brown or black I store them peeled in the freezer until the next time I feel like making banana bread. The agave makes this bread quite sweet; if that's not to your taste, consider substituting cocoa nibs for the chocolate chips. Other fruit or vegetable purées can be used—this also works with applesauce, and we make a delicious green tomato cake in the fall.

Makes one 9 x 5 x 3-inch loaf
Takes about 90 minutes

1 cup mashed bananas
2/3 cup agave syrup
1/2 cup vegetable oil
1 1/4 cup flour
1/4 cup bran
1 teaspoon baking soda
1 teaspoon cinnamon
1/4 teaspoon ground cloves
3/4 cup chocolate chips

Preheat the oven to 350°F.

Beat together the bananas, agave, and oil in a large bowl. They start out lumpy, but after a minute or two begin to combine and smooth. In a second bowl stir together the flour, bran, baking soda, cinnamon, and cloves.

Add the flour mixture to the wet ingredients and stir until they combine completely. Then add the chocolate chips and mix until they are well-distributed throughout the batter.

Grease a 9 x 5 x 3-inch loaf pan. Pour the mixture into it. Bake for 40–60 minutes, or until a skewer inserted into the center of the loaf comes out clean. Let the bread cool for 10 minutes or more before serving. Store your banananana bread in the fridge, or slice it and store it in the freezer.

COFFEE CAKE WITH CHILI-CHOCOLATE CRUMB

This is the sort of cake you'd expect to discover at a café. Serve it with coffee or brewed chocolate (page 29).

Makes one 9 x 13-inch cake
Takes 60 minutes

Base
2 1/4 cups flour
3/4 cup sugar
3/4 cup vegetable oil
1 teaspoon cinnamon
1/4 teaspoon salt

Chili-chocolate crumb
1/3 cup chopped nuts
1/4 cup sugar
2 tablespoons cocoa powder
1 1/2 teaspoons cinnamon
1 teaspoon chili flakes

Coffee cake
1 cup raisins
1 cup chopped walnuts or pecans
1 teaspoon chili powder
1 teaspoon baking powder
1 teaspoon baking soda
1 cup plant milk
1/4 cup applesauce or blended apple
2 tablespoons lemon juice or vinegar

Follow the instructions for the base, then the crumb, then the cake.

Base

Combine the flour, sugar, oil, cinnamon, and salt in a mixing bowl. The "crumb base" is 3/4 cup of this mixture. The "cake base" is what's left after the crumb base is removed.

Chili-Chocolate Crumb

Combine the crumb base, nuts, sugar, cocoa powder, cinnamon, and chili flakes.

Coffee Cake

Preheat the oven to 325°F.

Stir into the cake base the following ingredients: raisins, walnuts, chili powder, baking powder, and baking soda. Mix in the plant milk, applesauce, and lemon juice.

Pour the batter into a greased 9 x 13-inch baking pan. Gently press the chili-chocolate crumb onto the top of the batter. Bake for 35–40 minutes. Let the cake cool in the pan, then gobble it all up.

CHOCOLATE CARDAMOM MANGOES

I spent a summer working on a mango farm in tropical north Queensland, so we had access to more mangoes than we could eat. When I think of these chocolate cardamom mangoes, they remind me of so many tropical memories. Serve this over rice for breakfast or over ice cream and brownies for a sweet dessert.

Makes 2 half-mango servings
Takes 20 minutes

1 mango (slightly firm is good)
2 teaspoons ground cardamom, divided
1 teaspoon cocoa powder
1 tablespoon oil
2 teaspoons cocoa nibs, minced
1 teaspoon sugar

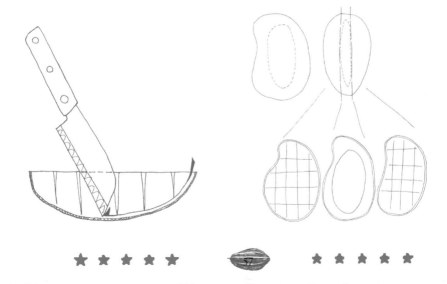

★ ★ ★ ★ ★   57   ★ ★ ★ ★ ★

Cut mango into halves and remove the seed. Slice a 1/2 inch grid into the meat of the mango halves, leaving the skin intact.

Sprinkle one teaspoon of cardamom and the cocoa powder over the gridded mango halves.

Warm the oil in a large pan over medium heat. Add the nibs, sugar, and the remaining cardamom to the pan. Scrape any flesh off the mango seed, mince it, and add it to the pan.

Put the mango halves in the pan flesh-side down and press down into the pan. Cook uncovered for 5 to 10 minutes, until they are heated through.

Turn off the heat and remove the mango halves from the pan to cool. When they have cooled enough to handle, invert the skins and scrape free any flesh that doesn't fall off. Drizzle the sauce from the pan over the mangoes and serve them while they're still warm.

CHOCOLATE CARDAMOM PEARS: If you don't have access to tropical fruit, substitute a pear for the mango. Cut the pear into 1/4-inch cubes. Toss them in a bowl with cocoa powder and one teaspoon of cardamom, then proceed with the recipe. Instead of pressing them into the pan, stir occasionally while cooking. Once they are hot and coated with the sugar mixture, transfer them directly to a bowl and drizzle them with sauce from the pan.

DATE BALLS

Add these date balls to a platter along with other finger foods and all of a sudden your platter is extra fancy. The more finely you mince, the more elegant these date balls will look in the end—and the better they'll hold together.

Makes 12 date balls
Takes 15 minutes

1 cup dates, pitted
1 tablespoon nibs
1 tablespoon shredded coconut
(optional)
About 20 pistachios (12 whole plus
1 tablespoon minced)

Mince all the ingredients except a dozen of the pistachios. Combine the minced pistachios, nibs, and coconut.

One tablespoon at a time, roll the dates into cylinders or balls. Press a pistachio into the center, and work the nut and nib mixture into your ball like you're breading it. That's all! Voila! Date balls!

DATE BALLS #2

I invented these while working on the original date balls, which were inspired by the coconut-date rolls found in the bulk section at our food co-op. You can make these in no time, and they look lovely in a glass jar. They get eaten so fast I wonder if I ever really made them.

Makes 15–20 bite-sized balls
Takes 15 minutes

1 cup minced dates
1 tablespoon minced sunflower seeds
1 tablespoon minced hazelnut
1 tablespoon minced cocoa nibs
1/2 teaspoon vanilla extract
Zest of one orange (optional)
2 tablespoons cocoa powder (for coating)

In a bowl, thoroughly mix together all the ingredients except cocoa powder.

A spoonful at a time, roll them into balls. We recommend tablespoon-sized balls, but this is not an exact science.

Sprinkle the balls with cocoa powder or drop them into a small bowl of cocoa powder and roll them around. The cocoa powder makes the balls less sticky, easier to handle, and prettier.

Store them in a container that keeps its shape; in a bag they'll get squished but still taste great.

THRILLING DATE BALLS: Find a chili powder with a super-high heat unit and make a few extra-spicy date balls. Share them with friends who are always seeking the hottest of spicy foods and they'll be thrilled.

TRAIL MIX DATE BALLS: You can make these date balls with all sorts of minced trail mix ingredients in place of the sunflower seeds and hazelnuts. Experiment! If you add too many nuts and you've run out of dates, sprinkle the extra mixture over oatmeal.

NANA'S CARROT CAKE FOR BIRTHDAYS
DOUBLE CHOCOLATE STYLE

Nana's Carrot Cake has been the Wick family birthday cake for a couple generations. Darin grew up on it and his father before him. This a cake so special it has even been known to turn up in the mail. I have been granted special permission from Darin to turn it into a chocolate carrot cake—as long as I promise not to call it a birthday cake, because the birthday version doesn't contain any chocolate. I always make substitutions in recipes, and I never get to play with Nana's Carrot Cake for Birthdays, so I enjoyed finally getting permission to alter this well-loved recipe.

Makes one 11 x 7-inch cake
Takes 45 minutes prep plus 60–65 minutes baking

1/2 cup raisins
1/2 cup currants (or more raisins)
1/2 cup chopped pecans or sunflower seeds
2 teaspoons cocoa liqueur (optional)
2 large carrots (about 2 1/2 cups grated)
1 1/2 cups unsifted all-purpose flour
2 teaspoons cinnamon
1/2 teaspoon allspice
1/2 teaspoon cloves
1/2 teaspoon nutmeg
1/2 teaspoon cardamom
1 1/2 teaspoons baking soda
1 1/2 teaspoons salt
1 cup unsweetened applesauce
1 1/2 cups white sugar
3/4 cup cocoa powder
1 cup vegetable oil
1 teaspoon vanilla extract
1/2 teaspoon grated fresh ginger (optional)
2–3 cups Aquafaba Cashew Chocolate Frosting (page 49)

Preheat the oven to 325°F. Mix the raisins, currants, and chopped pecans with the cocoa liqueur and set the mixture aside. Grate the carrots and set them aside, too.

Combine the flour, cinnamon, allspice, cloves, nutmeg, cardamom, baking soda, and salt. Mix it well and set it aside. In a large mixing bowl, beat in the applesauce, white sugar, cocoa powder, oil, vanilla, and ginger. Stir in the dry ingredients. Fold in the carrots, dried fruit, and nuts. Mix thoroughly.

Grease and flour the bottom of an 11 x 7-inch cake pan. Pour the mixture into the pan. Bake for 60–65 minutes or until a toothpick comes out fairly dry. Frost the cake with Goose's Aquafaba Cashew Frosting (page 50) and cool it in the pan.

CHOCOLATE-CURRY CARROT CAKE WITH CARDAMOM FROSTING: A friend gave this variation a rave review, so we felt compelled to mention it. Substitute curry spices for the cinnamon, allspice, cloves, nutmeg, and cardamom. Add cardamom to your favorite basic vanilla frosting, and frost the cake.

RANGER COOKIES **BY HEIDI TIMM**

We spent so much of the winter at Heidi's café writing this cookbook and eating the most amazing baked goods in the entire city. She was kind enough to share one of her recipes with us. So if you happen to have a friend with cows and chickens, or maybe you're actually freegan, this is our highlighted dairy recipe.

Heidi suggests that vegans can swap Smart Balance for the butter and replace the egg with a smashed ripe banana or 3 tablespoons of aquafaba.

Makes 15–20 cookies
Takes 45 minutes

1 cups unbleached all-purpose flour
1/4 cup whole wheat pastry flour
3/4 teaspoon baking powder
1/2 teaspoon baking soda
1/2 teaspoon salt
1 1/4 cups old-fashioned rolled oats
1 cup pecans, toasted and chopped
1 cup dried sour cherries, chopped coarse
8 ounces bittersweet chocolate, chopped into small pieces or chocolate chips
3/4 cup (12 tablespoons, 1 1/2 sticks) unsalted butter, softened but still cool
1 1/2 cups packed dark brown sugar
3 tablespoons of aquafaba or 1 extra large egg
1 teaspoon vanilla extract

Preheat oven to 350°F (175°C), with racks on the top and bottom thirds. Use parchment paper to line 2 sheet pans and set aside.

Pour dry ingredients into a bowl.

In another bowl combine the oats, pecans, dried cherries and chocolate.

In the mixer, cream together the butter and sugar on medium speed until light and fluffy, scraping down the sides of the bowl as needed. Slowly add the egg and beat until incorporated.

Gently sift, or with the mixer down to low, add the flour mixture to the bowl. Stir until just combined.

Finally incorporate the oats, nuts, fruit and chocolate with wooden spoon.

Use a 1/3 cup scoop, then press to 3/4 inch.

Bake the cookies, two trays at a time, for 12 minutes. Rotate at 6 mins. Cook until the cookies are uniformly golden, but still wet in the middle. They should appear slightly undercooked.

Remove from the oven and cool on the speed rack.

SALAD BROWNIES

This unique summer-fall hybrid was a bright idea that's so wrong it's exactly right. It looks like a brownie, but it tastes like a brownie salad.

If this is for a potluck, make the brownies ahead of time; they taste better the next day.

Makes one 8 x 8-inch baking pan
Takes 60 minutes

1 1/2 cups flour
1 cup sugar
1/2 cup oats
1/2 cup cocoa powder
1 teaspoon curry powder
1 1/2 teaspoons baking soda
1 teaspoon salt
2 cups shredded zucchini
1/2 cup applesauce
1/2 cup raisins (or dried cherries)
1/2 cup pumpkin seeds
1/2 cup chocolate chips
1/3 cup aquafaba (chickpea juice)
2 teaspoons vanilla

Preheat the oven to 350°F. In a mixing bowl, combine flour, sugar, oats, cocoa powder, curry powder, baking soda, and salt. Squeeze the excess liquid from the zucchini into a nearby houseplant. Mix in the zucchini, applesauce, raisins, pumpkin seeds, chocolate chips, aquafaba, and vanilla.

Pour the batter into a greased 8 x 8-inch baking pan. Cook in the oven for about 45 minutes; a fork will *not* come out mostly clean, so just keep them in the oven until you start to worry about them burning.

BROWNIE-BROWNIES: Substitute flour for the oats and walnuts for the pumpkin seeds and you'll get a brownie that is basically normal.

These brownies are on the cakey side, but you won't even notice the zucchini.

SIMPLE GIFT JAR

This quick and easy recipe was initially discovered by accident. It makes chocolate chips look like mini truffles, and these jars make great gifts.

We have tried adding assorted spices in place of the cocoa powder but for the most part they don't stick as well. We recommend sticking to cocoa on chocolate.

Makes one 4-ounce jar
Takes 10 minutes

Ingredients
1/2 cup chocolate chips
1/2 teaspoon cocoa powder

Materials
1 glass jar (4 ounces)
1 short length of ribbon (optional)
1 repurposed small rectangular paperboard, hole-punched (optional)

In the jar, combine all the chocolate chips and cocoa powder and put the lid on. Shake well.

Fold the paperboard in half, punch a hole in the top left corner, decorate the cover, and write a sweet note inside. Thread the ribbon through the card's hole and then use the ribbon to tie a bow around the neck of the jar. Voila! Fancy chocolate chips!

TAMARIND-GINGER BRAN MUFFINS

Ginger, orange, and tamarind add a delightful complexity to these muffins. As with so many foods, bran muffins are better with cocoa butter.

Makes 18–20 muffins
Takes 45 minutes

1 1/4 cups water
1 3/4 cups wheat bran
1 tablespoon ground flax seeds
2 1/4 cups flour
2 1/2 teaspoons baking soda
1/2 teaspoon salt
6 tablespoons melted cocoa butter
1 cup chopped nuts (use a softer nut, such as walnuts, pecans, or sunflower seeds)
1 cup dried fruits such as raisins or currants
2/3 cups molasses
1/4 cup applesauce
1/4 cup minced dates
3 tablespoons tamarind paste
3 tablespoons grated fresh ginger
1/2 teaspoon orange extract (or 1 teaspoon unwaxed orange zest, if available)

Preheat the oven to 400°F and put the water on to boil. Add the wheat bran and flax seeds to the boiling water and set aside.

Mix together the flour, baking soda, and salt in one bowl. Melt the cocoa butter. In a separate bowl, mix the cocoa butter, nuts, fruits, molasses, applesauce, dates, tamarind paste, ginger, and orange extract. Then combine all ingredients.

If your orange is at all pretty or shiny, the odds are good that it has a coat of wax on it, complete with fungicide. We favor orange extract over zest.Maybe you know someone with a tree?

Grease a muffin pan, then pour the mixture into the pan. Bake the muffins for about 15 minutes, or until a fork comes out fairly dry. Careful, they're hot!

If you somehow manage to have any leftover muffins, store them in an airtight container wrapped in a cloth napkin.

BY AMY BUGBEE

Oh emm gee, we love Amy Bugbee. She's a vanilla expert and talented cook to boot. She knocks these gluten-free cookies out of the park and we go scrambling to gather them all up.

Makes 16–20 cookies
Takes 40 minutes

2 cups almond flour
1/2 teaspoon baking soda
1/4 teaspoon sea salt
1/8 teaspoon ground cinnamon
1/3 cup pure maple syrup
3 tablespoons melted coconut oil
1 tablespoon vanilla extract
1/4 teaspoon almond extract
20 almonds
3–4 ounces dark chocolate

A SIMPLE DOUBLE-BOILER

Preheat oven to 325°F.

Combine almond flour, baking soda, salt, and cinnamon in a bowl. In a separate bowl, combine maple syrup, melted coconut oil, vanilla extract, and almond extract. Mix well. Pour wet ingredients into dry and stir until well combined.

Line a baking sheet with parchment paper and use a teaspoon to scoop batter onto it. Flatten the cookies a bit and top each cookie with an almond. Bake for 15 to 17 minutes or until lightly golden brown. Cool on a wire rack.

While the cookies are cooling, melt the chocolate in a double boiler. Once the cookies are completely cool, dip their bottoms in melted chocolate and place them on waxed paper to dry.

BONUS DESSERTS

Aquafaba: This magical new vegan egg replacer is chickpea juice. A lot of the foods you can make contain chocolate. Try the meringue! Garbanzo beans as a by-product? I see chocolate-beet hummus (page 88) in your future....

Avocado mousse: My friend made this and reports that it is amazing and not to be missed.

Brownies: Try searching for your favorite vegetable + brownie. Cauliflower, carrot, corn, beet, spinach & other greens, squashes... the possibilities are endless. You can hide so many different kinds of vegetables in brownies!

Chocolate salami: We discovered this while browsing Wikipedia for all things chocolate. Chocolate salami keeps up the appearance of a processed pig or cow, and it really looks just like salami! This is a mock meat in no other sense: cookies replace gristle and chocolatey goodness replaces the rest.

Fudge for breakfast: My grandma once told me that I get my sweet tooth from my grandpa. Early on in their marriage, she woke up one morning to find him at the kitchen table eating fudge for breakfast. Next time you make fudge, have some for breakfast. It's totally a thing.

German chocolate cupcake: Need we say more?

Marzipan: Marzipan is a sculptable paste made of ground almonds and sugar. It's often found dipped in chocolate, but you can also make it by adding ground nibs to the marzipan itself.

Sachertorte: This is a famous Viennese rich chocolate layer cake made with apricot jam and served with unsweetened whipped cream. It's so good that there was a drawn-out legal battle (back in the day) over who could claim it as their own invention.

Gluten-free chocolate cake: It's closer to a fudge, really, and that's why we love it.

Pudding: Chocolate pudding is the stuff of childhood. There are loads of chocolate puddings out there, with variations including coconut milk, tofu, and avocado. Try adding cocoa powder or nibs to a banana pudding!

Snobinettes: Our former landlord, Robert, is a semi-retired professional baker and a great person to live upstairs from. He taught us about snobinettes, which are edible chocolate bowls shaped using water balloons, which are then pierced once the chocolate solidifies. Fill them with fruit!

Tiramisu: We have an Italian friend who has insisted for as long as we've known him that he makes an amazing tiramisu and he really must make it for us. At this point, the status of his elusive tiramisu is so elevated in our minds that it's right up there with, well, chocolate.

SAUCES & SPREADS

CHILE SEASONING

Here is a theobrominated spin on a traditional Mexican treat. Sprinkle this powder on fruits and vegetables, add it to beans... the possibilities are endless.

Makes 1/2 cup
Takes 5 minutes

2 tablespoons sumac powder
2 tablespoons ground chile pepper
2 tablespoons cocoa powder
2 tablespoons ground cumin
1/2 tablespoon salt

Mix together all ingredients. Store in a jar and sprinkle on everything as needed.

FRESH LIME: During lime season, you can replace the sumac with the juice of a lime. This version must be refrigerated and should last for several days in the refrigerator.

CROCKPOT MOLE NEGRO

This smoky, nutty chocolate-based sauce is a relatively quick version of the real deal, which can take an entire day to prepare. I love crockpots for recipes like this. On the stovetop, it takes nearly an hour of supervised cooking. With an electric crockpot, I just need to prep a few hours earlier, and I can walk away until the mole is ready.

Mole is traditionally drizzled over burritos, enchiladas, or a variety of meats or meat-substitutes. It's like a complex, spicy barbecue sauce.

Makes 2 cups
Takes 1 hour prep plus 3 hours cooking (unattended)

3 tablespoons vegetable oil
1 medium onion, minced
3 cloves garlic, minced
1 teaspoon ground cumin
1/4 teaspoon ground cinnamon
1/4 teaspoon ground coriander
2 chipotles en adobo, seeded and minced (page 107)
1 tablespoon peanut butter
1 tablespoon chili powder or flakes
2 teaspoons cornmeal
1 teaspoon salt
3 cups vegetable broth
1 ounce dark chocolate, chopped (or about 1/4 cup grated chocolate)

Put a pan on medium heat and add the oil. When the pan is hot, add the onion and garlic and sweat them for fifteen minutes, stirring

occasionally. Add the cumin, cinnamon, and coriander, and cook them for another minute while stirring constantly.

Move the contents of the pan to a crockpot. Add the chipotles, peanut butter, chili powder, cornmeal, and salt. Stir in the broth and add the chocolate.

Cook in the crockpot on high heat for three hours. If you don't have a crockpot, simmer on medium heat for 50 minutes.

For a smooth texture, let the mole cool and blend it before serving. The mole can be refrigerated for up to two weeks, or kept frozen for several months. The oil separates out as it cools, but you can reheat the mole and stir it back in before serving.

CHOCOLATE CHILE BARBECUE SAUCE **BY GREG EVANS**

Greg made this barbecue sauce for a potluck and everyone loved it. We think you will, too.

Makes 2 cups
Takes 60 minutes

1 onion, diced
3/4 cup water
1/2 cup turbinado sugar
1/2 cup cider vinegar
3/4 cup (6 oz can) tomato paste
2 tablespoons unsweetened cocoa powder
1/2 teaspoon vanilla extract
1/2 teaspoon table salt
1/4–1/2 teaspoon chipotle powder (or more to taste, depending on how spicy you want it)

Sauté onion on medium heat until translucent and golden, about 20 minutes. Remove from skillet.

Add the water to the skillet and deglaze the pan by scraping and stirring; then add the sugar and simmer until the sugar dissolves. Pour into a blender or food processor along with the onions and the rest of the ingredients, and blend until smooth. Pour the resulting sauce back into a pan (or the same skillet) and simmer on low for 30 minutes.

EASY SAUCE: Essentially the same sort of sauce could be made more conveniently by using store-bought vegan barbecue sauce, adding the chocolate and chipotle powders to it, and simmering it for 20 minutes or so to let the flavors meld.

CHOCOLATE PEANUT BUTTER

I had a lot of fun working with Wendy Batterman on chocolate peanut butters. We learned just how subjective the sense of taste can be—I liked extra cocoa, while Wendy preferred more salt. If you use unsweetened peanut butter, the sugar will add a stronger chocolate flavor than the chocolate peanut butter would otherwise have. If your peanut butter already contains sugar, you can omit sugar from the recipe.

1 cup peanut butter
1/4 cup cocoa powder
Powdered sugar (optional)
Salt

In a jar, combine all ingredients and stir thoroughly. This can be a little messy. The alternative, also messy (but a little faster), is to combine all ingredients in a bowl and transfer the mixture to a jar using a rubber spatula.

Serve it on toast or sandwiches, use it as a base for a peanut sauce, or as a dip for fruits and vegetables. You can also mix in mini marshmallows, toasted coconut, granola, or other toppings.

★ ★ ★ ★ ★ ★ ★ ★ ★ ★

DAD'S STRAWBERRIES, CHOCOLATE STYLE

Strawberry season would come around when I was a kid, and I'd wake up one morning to sugared strawberries, which was the best surprise ever. My dad would make them by sprinkling sugar over strawberries and putting them in the fridge. I can even remember which container he would use. The sugar pulls the liquid out of the strawberries and you end up with syrupy strawberry goodness.

CARAMELIZED SUGAR

Preheat the oven to 300°F. Pour a bag of sugar into a glass baking pan and shake the pan so it's evenly distributed. Do not use a metal pan—that will melt the sugar instead of caramelizing it. Cook the sugar for 2–4 hours. Crush any chunks. Caramelization makes the sugar a little less sweet and more flavorful, which will result in a more complex strawberry dish. This will make a subtle difference for those with discerning taste buds.

This year, when strawberry season came around, I realized that we had no choice but to reinvent it. We eat this with pancakes, but it also goes well on peanut buttered toast.

Makes about 4 cups of strawberry topping (plus one mug of strawberry drink)
Takes all night (plus 2–4 hours baking the optional caramelized sugar)

4 cups sliced strawberries
1/3 cup chopped fresh mint leaves
6 tablespoons white
or caramelized sugar
2 tablespoons cocoa powder
1 teaspoon vanilla extract

In a large container, combine the strawberries, mint, sugar, cocoa powder, and vanilla extract. Put the lid on and put the container in the fridge. In the morning, it's ready! Use a fork to serve these strawberries over pancakes or toast.

FRESH, RICH STRAWBERRY DRINK: Drain the syrupy byproduct from the bowl of strawberries into a cup and add 1–2 times as much plant milk as there is syrup. Stir it, then sip it. This is objectively amazing and might be the best part of the whole "Dad's Strawberries" recipe.

STRAWBERRY SALSA: If you want something you can eat straight, decrease the sugar to 1/4 cup and replace the cocoa powder with 1/4 cup of cocoa nibs, and let it all sit for an hour instead of overnight.

GUACAMOLE

We had guacamole on a picnic one day and realized that we somehow *nearly forgot* to include cocoa guacamole in this book!(!!!) Darin even worked in Australia as a picker on an avocado and lime farm!

The roasted onion and corn are sweet, so they balance the bitter flavor of the cocoa powder.

Makes 2 cups
Takes 60 minutes

1 large tomato
1 small onion
2 chili peppers
1 ear's worth of corn (3/4 cup corn)
2 tablespoons vegetable oil
1 large avocado, ripe
1/4 cup cocoa nibs
Juice of one lime (2 tablespoons)
Salt

Preheat the oven to 375°F.

Chop the tomato, onion, and chili pepper. Put them and the corn on a baking pan and drizzle the oil over everything. Roast the vegetables for about 30 minutes, or until they start to turn a little brown at the edges.

Remove the roasted vegetables from the oven and put them in a bowl along with the avocado, nibs, and lime juice. Stir well and salt to taste. Voila! Guacamole is always best eaten fresh—even with lime, the avocado will oxidize. Serve with corn chips or eat straight from the spoon.

AWESOME BEAN DIP: Replace the avocado with 2 cups of refried beans, roast a few cloves of garlic with the other vegetables, and switch out the nibs for 3 tablespoons of cocoa powder.

HUMMUS OF THE GODS

The pinch of asafoetida—another "food of the gods," like chocolate—was just the thing this particular hummus needed to bring all the flavors together. This hummus makes a delightful treat for a potluck, and as a bonus, someone else will probably bring the vegetable sticks/chips/bread for dipping.

Consider making a double batch and storing half in the freezer for later so you don't have to make it as often.

Makes 2 cups
Takes 30 minutes

2 cups cooked garbanzo beans
1 small red beet, shredded
1/4 cup water
1 1/2 tablespoons tahini
1 1/2 tablespoons vegetable oil plus additional for garnish
1 1/2 tablespoons cocoa powder plus additional for garnish

★ ★ ★ ★ ★   88   ★ ★ ★ ★ ★

> Don't use much tahini? If you live near a grocery store with an extensive bulk section, bring a small container and buy just what you need.

1 teaspoon chili powder
1 teaspoon lemon or lime juice
1 teaspoon salt
Pinch of asafoetida powder
Cocoa nibs for garnish

Combine all ingredients, reserving any bean juice for recipes that require aquafaba. Blend the hummus for a smoother dip or mash by hand for a chunkier dip.

Serve with vegetable sticks and chips or bread.

DIVINE HUMMUS: Press a small indentation into the center of the hummus, and pour a puddle of vegetable oil into it. Sprinkle cocoa powder or nibs on top.

★ ★ ★ ★ ★ ★ ★ ★ ★ ★

ONION SPREAD

This rich chocolate-onion spread is great on sandwiches, and in pasta salads, potato salads, guacamole, and dressings. The spicy version makes a good substitute for chutney in lentil dishes. We use it as an ingredient to add flavor to all sorts of foods; see if it makes sense to add anywhere a recipe calls for cooked onion.

Makes about 3/4 cup
Takes 1 hour

2 tablespoons cocoa butter
1 large red onion, chopped
2 teaspoons cacao nibs
1/3 cup water
Salt

Put the cocoa butter and onion in a pan over medium-low heat. Cook the onion for about 40 minutes, or until it is translucent and mushy. Remove the onion from the pan and let it cool.

Once the onion has cooled, combine it with the nibs, water, and a pinch of salt. Blend it until the spread is smooth. It will last several weeks refrigerated or several months in the freezer.

SPICY ONION SPREAD: Substitute a white onion for the red onion. With the onion, cook a pinch of asafoetida powder, one minced chipotle pepper, and cumin seeds or a cinnamon stick. Remove the cinnamon stick after ten minutes.

PEANUT DIP

This tasty dip is based off an Aprapransa stew from Ghana. The original recipe called for a palm nut pulp, but we use peanut butter as it is more widely available in North America. Serve this dip with 1–2 cups of berries, apples, bananas, tomatoes, carrots, jicama, or other fruits and vegetables that go well with peanuts.

Makes plenty
Takes 60 minutes

1/4 cup vegetable oil
4 teaspoons annatto seeds
1 large onion
4 cups water, divided
2 cups cooked beans
1/4 cup peanut butter
4 medium tomatoes
1/2 cup uncooked polenta, or 1/4 cup corn flour
1/4 cup cocoa nibs
1/4 cup cocoa powder
2 tablespoons lemon juice
Salt

In a large saucepan over medium heat, briefly cook the oil and annatto seeds until the annatto seeds start to collect bubbles. Take the pan off the heat and wait a few minutes. Remove the seeds from the pan using a fork or a slotted spoon.

Mince the onion, then add it to the oil in the saucepan. Turn the heat back to medium and cook for about 15–20 minutes, or until the onion is translucent. Stir in the beans, one cup of water, and the peanut

butter. Dice the tomatoes, then stir them in along with another cup of water.

Start toasting the polenta in a small pan over medium heat, stirring constantly, for about five minutes or until it turns golden brown. Stir the polenta into the mixture along with another cup of water.

You can mince the cocoa nibs for a smoother dip and a more intense chocolate flavor. Stir in the cocoa nibs, cocoa powder, lemon juice, and remaining cup of water. Salt to taste.

Turn the heat down to low and stir occasionally until the dip is at your preferred consistency. For us, this takes about 10 minutes. Serve with fruits and/or vegetables.

SALSA PICANTE

Our housemate Bridget was so helpful when it came to understanding the names of these various salsas. We're not sure if she learned it growing up in Puerto Rico or raising a family in Texas, but she's a true salsa expert. Salsa is not a precise science; alter these recipes based on your preferences and what's in your kitchen. Remove the seeds from your peppers if you prefer a milder salsa.

Makes 3–4 cups
Takes 60 minutes

3 large tomatoes
1+ chili peppers
1 small onion
1 ear's worth of corn (3/4 cup)
2 tablespoons vegetable oil
1 medium tomatillo
1/4 cup chopped fresh cilantro (optional)
1/4 cup cocoa nibs
Juice of one lime (2 tablespoons)
Salt

Preheat the oven to 375°F.

Chop the tomatoes, peppers, and onion. Put them and the corn on a baking pan and drizzle the oil over everything. Roast them for about 30 minutes, or until they start to turn a little brown at the edges.

While the other vegetables roast, chop the tomatillo and cilantro. Remove the roasted vegetables from the oven, add the tomatillo, nibs, cilantro, and lime juice and stir well.

Salt to taste and serve with chips, add to burritos, or use it to make a taco salad.

SALSA VERDE: Replace 2 of the tomatoes with 2–3 medium tomatillos and 2 large green tomatoes. Add 1/4 cup of fresh mint, reduce the nibs to 2 tablespoons, and add 2 tablespoons of cocoa powder.

SALSA FRESCA: Follow salsa picante or salsa verde, but without roasting anything. Instead, chop the tomatoes, put them in a bowl, salt them, and set them aside. Drain and add the salted tomatoes. Use the salty tomato water in other dishes as salted water or vegetable broth.

VANILLA MOLE BY AMY BUGBEE

Mole comes in a variety of flavors, but it's the mole with cocoa in it that's famous. Mole is famously time-consuming to make, but you end up with a versatile, complex sauce that in this case, is vanillicious.

Makes enough mole to cover 1–2 pounds of tofu
Takes 3 hours, optionally let sit overnight

6 dried ancho, pasilla, or guajillo chiles, stemmed and
seeded
2 vanilla beans
1/2 cup sesame seeds, plus 1 tablespoon for garnish
1/2 teaspoon anise seeds
1/4 teaspoon cumin seeds
1/4 teaspoon coriander seeds
2 cloves or 1/8 teaspoon ground cloves
6 black peppercorns
1/4 teaspoon cinnamon
3 tablespoons vegetable shortening
1/4 cup raisins
1/2 cup raw pumpkin seeds or pine nuts
1 corn tortilla, quartered
5–6 tomatillos
5 garlic cloves, unpeeled
1 small onion, quartered
3 cups vegetable broth
2 ounces unsweetened chocolate, coarsely chopped
3 tablespoons maple syrup

Poblano chiles,
when dried, are
called anchos.

Chilaca chiles,
when dried, are
called pasillas.

Salt and freshly ground pepper
1–2 pounds tofu, sliced or cubed and fried until lightly browned on the outside
Quinoa or rice, prepared per package instructions
2 tablespoons chopped cilantro

In a medium bowl, cover the chile peppers and vanilla beans with hot water. Let them stand for 30 minutes.

In a large skillet, combine the 1/2 cup of sesame seeds with the anise, cumin, coriander, cloves, peppercorns and cinnamon. Toast over moderately low heat, stirring, until fragrant, about 2 minutes. Transfer to a spice grinder and let them cool completely. Grind the seeds and spices to a fine powder and set them aside.

In the same skillet, melt 1 tablespoon of the vegetable shortening. Stir in the raisins, pumpkin seeds, and tortilla. Cook the mixture over moderately low heat until seeds or nuts are toasted and the raisins are plump, about 5 minutes. Transfer the contents of the skillet to a large bowl.

Add the tomatillos to the skillet and cook, turning, until they are black on all sides and soft,

IN THE WILD, VANILLA VINES SOMETIMES CLIMB CACAO TREES.

A BRIEF HISTORY OF VANILLA
by Amy Bugbee

Imagine if you will the rain forests of tropical Veracruz, thick and shady, enjoying ocean breezes and mountain water. A small cacao tree grows shaded underneath the great canopy of taller green above, its vividly colored pods hanging. Woven up its trunk grows a leafy vine, a beautiful orchid, producing fleeting flowers, and, if the tiny Melipona bees reach them in time, long green fruits will hang heavy from it.

Vanilla had been cultivated as a staple for food, ceremony, and currency by ancient Mesoamericans long before the Aztecs conquered their lands, and an eternity before the Spaniards sailed up in the 1500s. Once Europeans got their hands on the vanilla bean they developed an unquenchable desire for the fragrant pods. It was coveted by kings and used as medicine to cure numerous ills and maladies.

Demand for the vanilla bean grew high, and this was a problem. The vanilla vine took years to produce a single flower, the flower bloomed for only a single day, and the bean took months to grow. Once the bright green bean was long and fat, it was picked, sun dried, and cured in a process that took many more months, and there was only so much to go around.

about 1-2 minutes. Transfer the blistered tomatillos to the bowl.

Add the garlic and onion to the skillet and cook, stirring, until lightly browned, about 8 minutes. Transfer the garlic and onions to the bowl and let cool along with the tomatillos, raisins, pumpkin seeds, and tortilla.

Once the contents of the bowl have cooled, transfer to a large cutting board. Peel the garlic cloves and coarsely chop along with everything else.

Melt 1 tablespoon of the vegetable shortening in the skillet. Stir in the ingredients that you have just chopped and add the spice powder. Cook over moderately high heat until warmed through, about 3 minutes.

Drain the chiles and vanilla beans, and add to the skillet

along with the veggie stock. Partially cover the skillet and simmer for 1 hour. Remove from the heat.

Remove vanilla beans.

Add chocolate and maple syrup. Let sit for 5 minutes or until chocolate melts.

Transfer the contents of the skillet along with the chocolate to a blender and puree until smooth. This may require more than one batch depending on the size of your blender.

Season the mole sauce with salt and pepper.

At this point you can let this sauce sit overnight to truly meld the flavors, or cook the tofu and prepare to serve it.

Money-hungry sea merchants snatched up the plants and attempted to grow them in tropical climates all over the South Seas, but returning even five years later they found nothing on the vines. Why? This was the question of the century, and the next century, and the next. It took literally hundreds of years for anyone to figure out the secret only the Melipona bee knew! It took until 1841, when Edmund Ablius, a 12 year old slave on the Reunion Islands, figured it out.

Edmund had cracked the code with a toothpick-size piece of bamboo. Even today, every single vanilla orchid is hand pollinated in exactly the same way! No machine can do this, only the agile hands of practiced farm workers. Drying and curing remains a lengthy process. Think of this the next time you see a vanilla bean, think of the luck of its being, and all of the ancient people and the people of today who have painstakingly aided in its existence, and how difficult and long its journey to reach you has been!

Brown tofu, pour mole over tofu and simmer.

Serve over quinoa or rice. Garnish with the remaining 1 tablespoon of sesame seeds and the cilantro and serve.

SPICED PEANUT BUTTER

This is another recipe made in collaboration with Wendy Batterman. It works well with a variety of powdered spice mixes—consider substituting karha masala, curry, 5-spice, pumpkin pie mix, or ras el hanout for the garam masala. Depending on whether it matches the spices you choose, add a little shredded coconut!

If you're opening a fresh jar of unmixed peanut butter, you can drain off the separated oil and use it to cook the spices.

1 cup peanut butter
1/4 cup cocoa powder
2 teaspoons peanut oil or olive oil
2 teaspoons garam masala
2 teaspoons shredded coconut (optional)
Powdered sugar (optional)
Salt

Gently sauté the spices and coconut with the peanut oil over medium-high heat to release the flavor of the spices. Let the sautéed spices cool for an elegant blending. Mix the spice blend in with the peanut butter, cocoa powder, sugar and salt.

BONUS SAUCES & SPREADS

Arugula pesto: This goes well with a little grated chocolate mixed in. Regular basil pesto and chocolate, maybe not so much. But this? Yes, this.

Baba ganoush: This is basically an eggplant hummus: roasted eggplant, tahini, garlic, lemon juice, salt. Make an indentation on top and fill it with a small pool of olive oil. Sprinkle pomegranate seeds, cumin, and cocoa powder and/or nibs in a decorative manner.

Chocolate fondue: A little messy for everyday snacking, fondue is great fun to share with friends. Bust out a collection of veggie sticks, for example, broccoli, carrots, golden beets, and jicama.

Chocolate tapenade: For some reason, this is almost the quintessential chocolate spread in my mind. It stands out as rich yet unique.

Cacao chutney: The sweet-and-spiciness of chutney usually balances bitter flavors in Indian cuisine. Add some nibs to your chutney and it's a whole new ball game.

Chocolate ketchup: There are like a million search results for this online, and it makes sense; the sweet & sour notes of the ketchup do well with the bitterness of cocoa. Give it a go!

Muhammara: A Turkish pepper dip, this goes well with bread. Grind some nibs along with walnuts when you make this. Cocoa powder works, too.

Mustard: Mustard spreads are a world unto themselves. Explore this world by adding variations on the cocoa theme!

Satsivi: I spent some time teaching English in the Republic of Georgia where they're very proud of their cuisine. You'll find versions of this walnut sauce used to fill bell peppers and to stuff rolls of sliced eggplant. Super fancy, super tasty. Add some nibs and have at it!

Vinaigrette: There is so much variety in these simple dressings! Start exploring by adding cocoa to mustard, berry, and chili-ginger vinaigrettes.

SOUPS, SALADS, & SNACKS

POZOLE

Pozole is a traditional Mesoamerican soup so old that it was said to be made in Aztec times with human flesh. These days, it's usually made with pig (which is apparently quite similar). This plant-based pozole is enhanced by a few unconventional ingredients.

Serve with tostadas, cabbage, onions, avocado, lime wedges, salad turnips, or radishes.

Makes 5 cups
Takes 60 minutes

2 tablespoons vegetable oil
1 large onion, chopped
2 chipotles en adobo, chopped
1 tablespoon tamarind paste
1/2 teaspoon cumin
2 cups cooked black beans
3 tablespoons cocoa powder
4 cups of vegetable stock
1 (14 ounce) can coconut milk
1 (15 ounce) can hominy
Soy sauce
Condiments (optional)

Put the oil in a soup pot over low heat, and stir in the chopped onion. Wander off and come back in 15 minutes. Add the chipotles, tamarind, and cumin and stir constantly for a few more minutes. Stir in the black

If you haven't bought hominy or chipotles en adobo before, look for them at a Mexican market or in the international aisle of a large grocery store. You can reserve the hominy water to make a corny cup of hot cocoa.

beans and cocoa powder and cook for another few minutes so that these flavors can all blend together.

Add the stock and coconut milk, increase the heat, and simmer for 10 minutes. Add the hominy and cook another 10 minutes. Season it to taste with soy sauce.

PUMPKIN SOUP

This sweet soup is a good choice for picky eaters on special occasions. Words cannot express how thrilled I would have been to receive this soup for dinner on my birthday as a child.

Makes about 6 cups
Takes 90 minutes

1 butternut squash
4 cups diced red onion
10 pods cardamom, crushed
5 whole cloves
1 cinnamon stick
1 1/2 tablespoons minced ginger
1 tablespoon coriander
1 teaspoon nutmeg
1 teaspoon vanilla
4 1/2 cups vegetable stock or water
1 (14 ounce) can coconut milk
1 (3 ounce) bar of dark chocolate
1 cup raisins
Pie crust (optional)

Preheat the oven to 375°F. Cut the squash in half, lengthwise, and place the halves face-down on a greased cookie sheet. Bake the squash for about an hour, or until it's soft enough to pierce easily with a fork. While the squash is in the oven, cook the onions in a large pot on low.

Stir the crushed cardamom, cloves, and cinnamon stick in with the onion. Stir occasionally.

By the time the squash is ready, the onion should be well caramelized. Stir in the ginger, coriander, nutmeg, and vanilla. Cook the onion-based mixture for a couple more minutes. Remove the skin from the butternut with a knife, chop the squash into chunks, and add them to the pot along with the vegetable stock and coconut milk.

Stir in the chocolate and continue stirring until the chocolate is melted. Use an immersion blender to blend the soup to a smoother consistency. Add the raisins, then simmer for another five minutes.

If you want to go all out, throw together a pie crust and serve it broken up on top of the soup like oyster crackers. *So good.*

SAVORY COCOA PUMPKIN SOUP

We were initially just going to include one pumpkin soup recipe, but we were having so much fun caramelizing the onions that we came up with two options. This savory version is our best solution to butternut season.

Makes about 6 cups
Takes 90 minutes

1 butternut squash
4 cups diced yellow onion
2 tablespoons cumin seeds
2 teaspoons mustard seeds
1 tablespoon powdered coriander
1 tablespoon curry powder
2 chile peppers
4 cups vegetable stock
2 cups plant milk
1 (3 ounce) bar of dark chocolate
2/3 cup pumpkin seeds
Pumpernickel bread (optional)

Preheat the oven to 375°F. Cut the squash in half, lengthwise, and place the halves face-down on a greased cookie sheet. Bake the squash for about an hour, or until it's soft enough to pierce easily with a fork. While the squash is in the oven, cook the onions in a large pot on low.

Stir in the cumin seeds and mustard seeds. Chop the chili peppers and roughly chop the chocolate.

By the time the squash is ready, the onion should be well caramelized. Add the coriander, curry powder, and chile peppers to the pot. Remove the skin from the butternut with a knife, chop the squash into chunks, and add them to the pot along with the vegetable stock and plant milk.

Stir in the chocolate and continue stirring until the chocolate has melted. Use an immersion blender to blend the soup to a smoother consistency. Add the pumpkin seeds. Serve with a side of pumpernickel bread.

STONE SOUP

This is the sort of recipe where you can add or substitute any vegetables that need to be saved from a rotten future. Turn the freezer inside out looking for that forgotten bag of green beans and rescue that rubbery carrot from a future decomposing in the compost bin. Use that rock-hard bit of ginger that has been in the fridge for aeons. Substitute fresh ingredients for powdered and powdered ingredients for fresh.

Makes about 4 cups
Takes 40–60 minutes

3 tablespoons oil
2 teaspoons cumin
1 teaspoon diced chili pepper
1 large onion, chopped
1 head of garlic
1/3 cup cocoa powder
2 teaspoons powdered turmeric
1 teaspoon chopped fresh ginger
1 cup chopped fresh mushrooms
1/2 cup peanuts or cashews, chopped
1/3 cup raisins
1 1/2 tablespoons tomato paste
4 cups soup stock or water
1/4 cup cilantro, chopped
Salt
Stale bread or cooked grains (optional)

Put the oil, cumin, and pepper in a large saucepan* over medium heat. After 1–2 minutes, add the onion. When the onion starts to look translucent, stir in the garlic, cocoa, turmeric, and ginger.

After the onions are cocoa-turmeric in color, add the mushrooms, peanuts, raisins, and finally the tomato paste. Add the stock and let the soup simmer for 20 minutes.

If you like a chunky soup, you're done; stir in the cilantro. If you prefer a creamier soup, add the cilantro and then blend the soup with an immersion blender. Salt to taste, and serve over a hunk of stale bread, or whatever abandoned grain left to your cupboard's farthest reaches.

*We totally just went back and forth over whether a "saucepan" was a pan or a pot. The internet solved our debate. A saucepan is illustrated for your edification.

FROM LEFT TO RIGHT: A POT, A SAUCEPAN, AND A PAN

STONE STEW: Omit the soup stock and stale bread. Try it; we liked it!

BUDGET SPINACH SALAD

This salad can be thrown together quickly using cocoa nibs and common kitchen staples. Since this is a budget salad, definitely substitute any greens, fruits, and nuts you already have handy.

Makes one bowl
Takes 10 minutes

1 cup coarsely chopped fresh spinach
1/4 cup raisins
1/4 cup sunflower seeds
2 tablespoons cocoa nibs
2 tablespoons vegetable oil
1 1/2 teaspoons lemon juice (or apple cider vinegar)
1/4 teaspoon salt

Toss all ingredients and serve. Rinse bowl, repeat.

Did you know the word "salad" comes from "salt"?

FANCY SPINACH SALAD

Sometimes, when I'm falling asleep at night, I'll describe the dreams I'm about have. One night, I fell asleep describing this dish. Be sure to use a bowl that's large enough for tossing!

Makes one bowl
Takes 20 minutes

2 tablespoons olive oil
2 tablespoons dried cranberries
1 1/2 teaspoons lemon juice
1 cup roughly chopped fresh spinach
2 tablespoons pine nuts, divided
2 tablespoons sweet nibs (page 123)
1 orange

Combine the oil, cranberries, and lemon juice and let them sit for 15 minutes.

In a bowl, add the mixture to the spinach and one tablespoon of the pine nuts, and toss everything well. At this point, if you're really going for fancy, transfer the salad to a fresh dish.

Sprinkle the sweet nibs and remaining pine nuts on top of the salad. Cut the orange using the most decorative technique you know (we like the double twist) and use it on the salad as an ornate garnish.

WINTER SALAD

This basic winter salad is great for everyday eating. It's chock full of nutrient-rich winter vegetables. The root vegetables add a little sweetness, and the nibs add a hint of pizzazz.

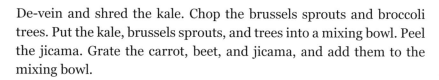

Makes about 2 cups
Takes 15 minutes

2 large leaves kale
3 brussels sprouts or 1/2 cup shredded red cabbage
1/2 cup chopped broccoli trees
1 small jicama
1 large carrot
1 small golden beet
2 tablespoons cocoa nibs
3 tablespoons oil
2 1/2 teaspoons lemon juice
Salt

De-vein and shred the kale. Chop the brussels sprouts and broccoli trees. Put the kale, brussels sprouts, and trees into a mixing bowl. Peel the jicama. Grate the carrot, beet, and jicama, and add them to the mixing bowl.

Add the cocoa nibs, oil, and lemon juice. Mix well and salt to taste. Serve this salad raw, pickle it to make kraut, or cook it by roasting, steaming, or stir frying.

GINGER BLISS: Replace the oil and lemon with 1/4 cup of coconut milk and 2 tablespoons of minced ginger.

CABBAGE ROLLS

These little packets work well as an appetizer or side at potlucks. The bitterness of the cocoa contrasts nicely with sweet steamed cabbage leaves, and the rice and lentils make it filling. Use a large-leafed cabbage if you can; it will make it easier to wrap up the rolls. They can be made ahead and served warm or cold.

Makes about 12 rolls
Takes 1 hour

2 tablespoons vegetable oil
1 small onion
2 cloves garlic
2 cups vegetable stock
1/2 cup dry lentils
1/2 cup brown rice
1/3 cup nibs
Salt and pepper
1 head of cabbage

Put oil in a saucepan on low heat. Mince the onion and add it to the pan. Cook for 10–15 minutes, stirring occasionally, until it's translucent. Mince the garlic, stir it in, and cook for another minute, then add stock.

When the water boils, add the lentils and rice. Simmer for about 30 minutes until most of the liquid has been absorbed. Add the nibs. Salt and pepper the mixture to taste.

Cut the conical core out of the bottom of the cabbage and remove about a dozen of the large outer leaves, being careful not to tear them. Leaves on older or smaller cabbages can be hard to remove without tearing, but they can be softened and loosened by steaming for 10 minutes.

Steam the leaves for about 15 minutes until they begin to bend easily. If thick stems prevent the leaves from rolling, cut a V-shaped section of stem out of each leaf. Put a few tablespoons of filling on each leaf, fold the sides in, and roll them into miniature cabbage-burritos.

Stack the rolls, seam-side down, in a steamer over a few inches of water. Bring the water to a boil, and cook for 10–15 minutes.

DRIED CANTALOUPE

This recipe requires a dehydrator! If the weather is hot and sunny, research solar dehydrating—it can be as simple as a few screen trays.

We discovered driead cantaloupe through a happy accident: a tasty-smelling melon was mushily overripe, the dehydrator was already running... and it turned out surprisingly well! Depending on how long you leave the melon in the dehydrator it will become chewy like dried mango or turn into crisp cantaloupe chips. Add a little spiced cocoa and *boom!* Magic.

Makes about 10 pieces of cantaloupe jerky
Takes 20 minutes prep (drying time depends on your dehydrator)

1 small cantaloupe
2 teaspoons cocoa powder
1 1/2 teaspoons minced fresh ginger
1/2 teaspoon chili flakes (optional)
1 tablespoon lemon juice

Stir together the cocoa powder, ginger, chili flakes, and lemon juice to form a thin paste. Cut the cantaloupe in half and scoop out the seeds. Cut each half into 1/4"-thick pieces and slice off the rinds. Coat one side of each slice with the chocolate paste and dry according to your dehydrator's instructions.

Check the slices periodically, since different dehydrators can have vastly different drying times. Leave the cantaloupe in the dehydrator until beads of water don't form when it is torn.

Dehydrated fruit can last many months in an airtight container, or even longer if stored in the fridge or freezer.

BROCCOLI TREES

When I was a child, I loved to pretend that broccolis were miniature trees. We wanted to highlight how to use cocoa butter for a subtle cocoa flavor when sautéing, and broccoli qua broccoli was a natural choice.

Makes about two cups, or 800 tiny nibbles
Takes 10 minutes

1 head broccoli, chopped
1/3 cup vegetable stock
1 tablespoon cocoa butter
1 teaspoon minced ginger
Salt

In a saucepan, combine the broccoli, stock, cocoa butter, and ginger. Sauté your trees by cooking them over medium-high heat while tossing everything for about 5 minutes. Salt to taste.

Serve over rice or eat it straight from the pan.

STRAWBERRY-MINT SANDWICH

We were at a cafe working on this very cookbook, minding our own business. When we overheard someone order a savory sandwich, I had to ask the question: "What would a sweet sandwich look like?" As it happened, strawberries were in season, so we went home and tested our theory. This strawberry-mint sandwich is delicious and we recommend making it with fresh, thinly-sliced rye bread.

Makes one sandwich
Takes 10 minutes

3 medium strawberries
2 slices of bread
2 tablespoons grated chocolate
Mint leaves to cover a slice of bread
2 teaspoons cocoa butter, divided

Slice the strawberries and lay them out in a single layer on one slice of bread. Sprinkle the grated chocolate over the strawberries, cover everything with a layer of mint leaves, and close your sandwich with the second slice of bread.

Place half of the cocoa butter in a skillet over medium heat. Put the sandwich on top of the pat of cocoa butter so that the fat will soak into the bread rather than spread around the pan. Cover the skillet and cook the sandwich for about two minutes, or until the bottom of the sandwich begins to turn golden-brown. Flip the sandwich, placing the remaining cocoa butter under the sandwich, and cook for another two minutes, covered.

Serve while it's hot from the pan.

SWEET NIBS BY JANET STRAUB

Janet, the official "Chocolate Doodler" of Creo Chocolate, suggests using nibs anywhere you'd use nuts or seeds. The parchment paper in this recipe is handy because it makes cleanup straightforward. These candied nibs go great on salads!

Makes 1 1/2 cups
Takes 10 minutes

1/4 cup sugar
2 tablespoons water
1 1/2 cups cacao nibs

Over medium low heat, stir the sugar and water until the sugar is dissolved and the mixture thickens slightly. This takes less than 2 minutes. Remove from heat and stir in the nibs until evenly coated. Pour onto parchment paper to cool and dry out. Store in an airtight container.

Use these sweet nibs as a snack, in salads, and creatively topping food.

BONUS SOUPS, SALADS, & SNACKS

While chocolate can be used all year long, most people seem to think of chocolate during the winter months. Soup is the same way! So add some cocoa to your favorite soup and you've got a cozy new winter tradition. We also want you to know that cocoa nibs and salads go together like salt and pepper. Add nibs to most everyday salads. Or add cocoa buttered croutons! Substitute cocoa butter and otherwise make them like you'd make regular croutons.

Borscht: Borscht is a sweet and sour soup. Add some nibs and compensate for their bitterness with a little extra sweetness (like a few extra carrots).

Chocolate jalapeño corn bread: Sweet, spicy, and bitter: these flavors are super matchy, so if you like the ingredients, we recommend that you whip up a batch.

Fig, fennel & almond salad: Combine fresh figs, fresh fennel, sliced almonds, cocoa nibs, butter lettuce, olive oil, and champagne vinegar. Salt to taste. Almonds in agriculture require a lot of water to grow beyond rainfall requirements, but it's a flavor classic that bears mentioning.

Jicama: Slice a medium jicama into rounds and top with Mexican chile seasoning (page 89)

Nibby trail mixes: We're all about the trail mixes. They pack so well! They're such a great way to make sure we eat our nuts and seeds! With trail mix, there's so much room for creativity and variety. Nuts, seeds, dried fruits, optional coconut flakes, and cocoa nibs or chocolate chips. Go nuts!

Spiced garlic bread: Make a roasted garlic cocoa butter with spices that tie together the flavors of garlic and cocoa butter. Then use the garlic butter to make garlic bread.

Spicy popcorn: Throw your favorite spices (or try chili pepper, cumin, or cinnamon) in a pan with a mix that's half vegetable oil and half cocoa butter, then pour it all over a bowl of popcorn. Use a spray bottle to add a little lemon juice or watered-down tamarind paste to the popcorn.

Split pea soup: Make it with chile peppers, ginger, and nibs.

MAIN
COURSES

BRUSSELS SPROUTS WITH CARAMELIZED ONION

These Brussels sprouts are a December recipe, so when we add the citrus to this I'm reminded of my childhood in England, where candy and candle-decorated oranges called Christingles were part of a public school Christmas celebration.

The sweetness of the citrus and caramelized onion work well with the bitterness of the cocoa nibs and Brussels sprouts. Remember to start making the rice about halfway through this recipe if you don't already have some handy in a rice cooker!

Makes about 2 cups
Takes 60 minutes

1 tablespoon oil
1 large red onion, chopped
10 small Brussels sprouts, chopped
1/4 cup water
1 tablespoon dried mint
1 tablespoon cocoa nibs
1 orange or mandarin, separated into wedges
Salt and pepper
Cooked rice (optional)

Add the oil and onion to a pan and cook on medium heat for half an hour, stirring occasionally. Stir in the Brussels sprouts, add 1/4 cup water, and continue cooking for another 15–20 minutes, stirring rarely. When you can't take it anymore and just have to eat the deliciousness that awaits, remove from heat, and add the mint and nibs.

Brussels sprouts on
the stalk

Add salt and pepper to taste, serve over rice, and garnish with the orange wedges.

Invented in Germany in 1747, Christingles were popularized by the Children's Society in England in the late 1960s.

COCOA CURRY

I learned to make this in a hostel in Tropical North Queensland. As I stood in the kitchen cooking pasta, I peered over the shoulder of the person cooking on the next burner. Hostels are such a fun way to learn firsthand what people make as their own personal easy-to-cook food. Turns out my dad likes to learn how to cook new foods this way, too! Put brown rice on to cook before you start the curry, and remember to check your lentils for pebbles!

Makes about 2 1/2 cups
Takes about 40 minutes

1/4 cup vegetable oil
2 tablespoons garam masala
1 large onion, chopped
1 cup red lentils
2 tablespoons cocoa powder
2 cups water or vegetable broth
Salt
Cooked rice (optional)

Put the oil and garam masala in a small pot over medium heat. Cook them for 1–2 minutes, until it smells delicious, then add the onion. Stir occasionally.

After 5–10 minutes, stir in the lentils and cocoa powder. Cook for another five minutes, then add the water. Continue stirring occasionally. Cook for another 20 minutes, or until the lentils are mushy—that's the technical term for "soft and have lost their shape."

Salt to taste and serve over rice.

COCONUT CARDAMOM RICE WITH HIPS AND NIBS

I like this coconut rice because it's delicious, subtle, and so simple to make. It's especially easy with a rice cooker. This rice works best as a side rather than as a stand-alone dish.

Makes 1 1/2 cups
Takes 35 minutes

1 cup water
1/2 cup white rice
1/4 cup coconut cream
1 tablespoon cocoa nibs
1 teaspoon deseeded rose hips
1 teaspoon dried mint
1 teaspoon sugar
1/2 teaspoon powdered cardamom

CARDAMOM POD

Put all the ingredients in a rice cooker and cook until done. If you don't have a rice cooker, put everything in a covered pot over medium heat and simmer for about 20 minutes, or until the rice is done. Let it sit, still covered, for a few minutes. Fluff the rice and serve.

CHOCOLATE CARDAMOM RICE: Add 2 tablespoons of grated chocolate (or substitute for the sugar and nibs).

RICE PUDDING: Combine the diced peach, 1/4 cup raisins, and 1 teaspoon vanilla. Soak for at least an hour, then add them to the main recipe.

CREAMY CHOCOLATE OATMEAL

Chocolate oatmeal is basically the best breakfast ever. Fruits, nuts, and seeds are not optional unless you want to be hungry an hour later.

Makes 1 to 1 1/2 cups
Takes 20 minutes

SPICED APPLE

1 cup water
1/2 cup rolled oats
1/4 cup chopped apple (if dried, add a little extra water)
1/4 cup chopped walnuts or filberts
1 tablespoon cocoa nibs
1/2 teaspoon cinnamon
1/2 teaspoon allspice (optional)
1/4 teaspoon nutmeg (optional)
Plant milk (optional)

BUDGET OATS

1 cup water
1/2 cup rolled oats
1/4 cup raisins
1/4 cup sunflower seeds
1/4 cup coconut flakes (optional)
1 tablespoon cocoa powder
1/2 teaspoon vanilla extract (optional)
Plant milk (optional)

EXTRA-STRENGTH

1 cup water
1/2 cup rolled oats
1/2 cup seasonal fresh fruit
1/4 cup fresh nuts or seeds
2 tablespoons cocoa nibs
2 teaspoons cocoa powder
Plant milk (optional)

Combine all the ingredients of your preferred variation except the plant milk in a small pot, and cook on the stove at low heat. Stir occasionally, and add in a little more water if needed. Remove the pot from the heat after the oatmeal has simmered for about ten minutes, or when it is at your preferred texture, and serve hot. If it pleases you, add a little plant milk to your bowl of oats to cool it off.

INSTANT OATMEAL: Substitute quick oats for the rolled oats and dump everything—except for the water and plant milk—into a large bowl the night before. In the morning, stir in boiling water and wait a few minutes. Once you figure out your favorite combination, premix a large batch of the dry ingredients ahead of time.

PANTRY RESCUE: For all or part of the rolled oats, substitute that grain you got in the bulk aisle that one time. Adjust your cook time accordingly.

CHILI TODAY

Corn has a million industrial uses, and you can use more than just the kernels at home, too. Save corn husks for tamales or add them to your next batch of soup stock. If your corn came from a can and its ingredients are simply corn, water, and salt, you can use that corn water to replace some of the vegetable stock in this recipe. If you're attending a pun potluck, save the corn husks to make hot tamales and bring the two dishes together.

Makes about 2 cups
Takes 75 minutes

2 tablespoons vegetable oil
1 large yellow onion, diced
2 tablespoons cumin seeds
2 ears of shucked corn (or the corn from one 15-ounce can)
1 large tomato
2 chile peppers
1/2 cup grated baking chocolate (about 2 ounces)
1 1/2 cups cooked black beans
1 cup vegetable stock
1/4 cup fresh cilantro
Salt
Cornbread (optional)

Put the oil in a large pan over medium low heat. Add the onion and cumin seeds to the pan and stir them occasionally for fifteen minutes. Meanwhile, shell the corn—cut the corn kernels off the cob. Chop the tomato, dice the peppers, and grate the baking chocolate.

Put the beans and vegetable stock in a pot to simmer along with the corn, tomatoes, peppers, and chocolate.

Simmer on low for 30–45 minutes. Chop the cilantro, add it to the pot, and salt to taste. Serve with cornbread.

CHOCOLATE CAULIFLOWER GRATIN
BY FREDERICK LENZA

Frederick brought this innovative dish to our first "chocoluck," a chocolate potluck where everyone brought a dish made with cocoa and we all sat around eating theobrominated deliciousness. It was a smash hit with everyone who attended. It's good on its own, and it's also great in crêpes.

Fills one 9" round baking dish
Takes about 90 minutes

CAULIFLOWER
2 smallish heads of cauliflower, coarsely chopped
4 tablespoons peanut oil
1 tablespoon black pepper

SAUCE
1 tablespoon peanut oil
3 ounces Soyrizo
1 1/2 ounces baking chocolate
2 tablespoons flour
1 1/4 cups vegetable stock
1/4 cup red wine
1/2 tablespoon ponzu sauce (citrus-infused soy sauce)
1/4 teaspoon five-spice powder
1/4 teaspoon Moroccan seasoning (optional)
1/8 teaspoon liquid smoke

TOPPING
3 slices rye bread
2 tablespoons black truffle oil

CAULIFLOWER

Preheat the oven to 450°F. Toss cauliflower with 4 tablespoons peanut oil and black pepper. Put in roasting pan and roast at 450°F for 25 minutes, mixing the cauliflower again half way through.

SAUCE

Heat skillet to medium high heat. Add peanut oil. Crumble and fry soyrizo in oil until slightly browned and some fat has rendered, 5–10 minutes.

Decrease heat to medium. Melt chocolate into Soyrizo. Once chocolate has melted, add flour. Continue stirring to avoid scorching. Cook an additional 2 minutes to cook the taste of raw flour out of the roux.

Add vegetable stock, stirring constantly. Add red wine. Add ponzu sauce, five spice powder, Moroccan seasoning and liquid smoke. Simmer for 5 minutes to bring everything together; turn off heat.

TOPPING

Turn the bread into bread crumbs using either a grater or food processor. Toss with truffle oil.

ASSEMBLY

Preheat oven to 350°F. Take 9-inch round baking dish and combine the sauce with the roasted cauliflower. It should be enough to give a good coating to all the cauliflower. Mix well. Pack the mixture as tightly and evenly into the dish as possible. Sprinkle the topping on top of the casserole.

Bake at 350°F for 45 minutes. Place under broiler briefly until top is crunchy. Serve hot.

CHOCOLATE CHIP BLUEBERRY PANCAKES

When we want something special for breakfast, we turn to pancakes. One of the best parts is blueberries *and* chocolate chips in every pancake. For extra bonus fun, bust out the metal cookie cutters.

The basic ingredients in this pancake recipe are flour, baking powder, plant milk, and applesauce. If you just ran out of cloves or picked the last of your blueberries, or maybe plain forgot to add the sugar and oil like someone I know (*me*), they'll still come out pretty good.

Makes a mess and 12 pancakes
Takes 30–60 minutes

1 heaping cup flour
2 teaspoons baking powder
1 teaspoon cinnamon
1/2 teaspoon allspice
1/2 teaspoon nutmeg
1/4 teaspoon ground cloves
1 cup blueberries
1 cup plant milk
2/3 cup chocolate chips
1/2 cup applesauce or puréed apple
2 tablespoons vegetable oil
2 tablespoons sugar
1 teaspoon grated fresh ginger
1 teaspoon vanilla extract
Additional oil for cooking

Combine the flour, baking powder, cinnamon, allspice, nutmeg, and cloves in a large bowl. Mix well, then stir in the blueberries, plant milk, chocolate chips, applesauce, oil, sugar, ginger, and vanilla extract.

Warm an oiled skillet over medium heat. Use a ladle or a 1/4-cup measuring cup as a scoop to pour the batter into the pan. Fry for 2–4 minutes, or until bubbles show up in the pancake, then flip the pancake and cook it for another 1–2 minutes. Eat straight from the pan or politely serve in a stack on a plate.

PB & J PANCAKES: To bring these pancakes back down to earth, replace the allspice, nutmeg, cinnamon, ginger, blueberries and chocolate chips with a 1/4 cup of cocoa powder and 2 teaspoons of garam masala, and serve them with peanut butter and jelly. This makes enough sturdy pancakes for a week's worth of pancake-based PB & J sandwiches.

SAUCY ROASTED EGGPLANT

This easy eggplant dish gets rave reviews at potlucks. The cocoa is used as a subtle spice, but for a bolder chocolate flavor you can use 1/4 cup of cocoa powder and increase the sugar to one tablespoon.

Makes one 8 x 13-inch cake pan
Takes 60 to 90 minutes

1 eggplant (about 1 pound)
13.5 ounces of coconut milk (about 2 cups)
2 cups diced tomatoes
2 tablespoons cocoa powder
4 teaspoons ras el hanout or garam masala
2 teaspoons sugar
1/2 teaspoon salt

Did you know?
Eggplant gets its name from the white variety that is shaped like an egg.

Preheat the oven to 350°F. Cut the eggplant into slices up to 1/4" thick and put a single layer in the bottom of an oiled 8 x 13-inch cake pan.

Mix together the coconut milk, diced tomatoes, cocoa powder, ras el hanout, sugar, and salt in a medium bowl. Evenly distribute about half the sauce over the eggplant. Add the remaining eggplant slices as a second layer, and then pour all the remaining sauce on top.

JAPANESE AND EUROPEAN EGGPLANTS

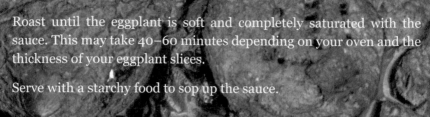

Roast until the eggplant is soft and completely saturated with the sauce. This may take 40–60 minutes depending on your oven and the thickness of your eggplant slices.

Serve with a starchy food to sop up the sauce.

FANTASTIC BURRITO FILLING OR BEAN DIP: Keep any sauce that remains after baking. Add the sauce to a couple cups of cooked black beans and heat it on the stove for 5–10 minutes. If you mash the beans while cooking them, it also makes a great bean dip.

This is mashed potatoes like you've never had them before. You can experiment with the recipe by using chocolate bars with different cacao contents (we used 70% cacao), and you can add more cranberry sauce than we call for at your discretion. The end result looks like a bean dip. Serve this sweet dish anywhere you'd serve mashed potatoes with gravy.

Makes 3 cups
Takes 20 minutes

3 cups of potatoes or yams
1 (3 ounce) plain dark chocolate bar
1/2 cup cranberry sauce or jam

Set a small pot of water on to boil. While the water is heating, dice the potatoes and add them to the water. When the potatoes are soft enough to be cut with a fork, remove them from the heat and strain them. Break up the chocolate bar and stir it into the potatoes until it is entirely melted and the potatoes are at your desired consistency. Stir in the cranberry sauce, but stop before it is fully mixed in so that you end up with cranberry swirls.

STUFFING

Stuffing is a crucial—and coveted—part of our autumn feasts. This particular stuffing has been a huge hit at potlucks. Serve alongside the mashed potatoes on page 143.

Makes 3–4 cups
Takes 30 minutes

4 thick slices of bread
1/2 cup shredded kale
1/2 cup shredded red cabbage
1/2 cup diced dates
1/4 cup cacao nibs
1/4 cup vegetable oil
2 tablespoons apple cider vinegar
Salt

Toast the bread. Mix the kale, cabbage, dates, nibs, oil, and vinegar in a large bowl.

Soak the bread in water for about three minutes, then wring it out like a wet towel and crumble it into the other ingredients. Toss everything together and salt to taste.

Let the stuffing sit for 20 minutes before serving.

SUNSET WHEAT BERRY SALAD

BY ANGELA PILLER[2]

Angela brought this sweet, wholesome salad to our chocoluck and everyone really enjoyed it. I didn't even think I liked wheat berries, but it was so good that I ate every last bite.

Makes 3 cups
Takes 10 minutes

SALAD

4 Fuyu persimmons, peeled and sliced
1/3 cup pecans, chopped
1/4 cup cocoa nibs
1/3 cup raisins
2/3 cup cooked wheat berries

DRESSING

1 tablespoon honey
1 tablespoon orange juice
1 1/2 teaspoons cocoa powder
1/2 teaspoon cinnamon
1/4 teaspoon salt

Combine all salad ingredients in a large bowl. Combine dressing ingredients and whisk. Pour dressing over salad and gently toss. Enjoy!

Persimmons are in season during the fall and winter. This is easy to remember because they are very striking on the tree when in fruit. Persimmons are ripe, bright-orange ornaments during the grey time of year when the trees have lost all their leaves.

Contains honey

BONUS MAIN COURSES

Bean dishes: Chocolate goes well with a wide variety of bean dishes. Start with Spanish rice and beans con cacao and then try everything else, too!

Burritos: Leftovers go great in burritos. Make a little extra of something else and use the surplus to stuff a tortilla. Add standard burrito ingredients as needed.

Cocoa pasta: While this is common enough that you can buy it premade, we were unable to find a fair trade version. Fortunately, making chocolate pasta is a fun project to share with a friend!

Penne with peas: Take a pound of plain penne pasta, cook it, add a bag of frozen peas along with cocoa nibs, aquafaba mayonnaise, and unblended onion spread (page 91). This is a dish best served cold.

Sandwiches: Use chocolate onion spread (page 91) on all sorts of veggie-based sandwiches, or use spiced peanut butter (page 102) to make a PB&J.

Stir-fried veggies: Stir fry whatever is in season. When the veggies are cooked, stir in chunks of chocolate until they melt.

Stuffed capsicums: Stuff and roast bell peppers and stuffable chili peppers with all sorts of cocoa-based fillings. For example, stuff red bell peppers with coconut rice, nibs, and mango. Garnish by sprinkling toasted coconut on top.

Tamales: They take a while to cook—plan at least two hours for a medium-size batch—but tamales are delicious, and a perfect food to freeze for future snacking. You can mix chocolate into regular masa, or use cacao in the filling.

Until the mid-1800s, everyone who consumed chocolate was drinking a variation on the same beverage first tasted by pre-Olmec peoples. As Julianna Labruto of Diego's Chocolate told us, modern chocolates—bars, truffles, and the lot—are a distinctly industrial product.

Solid chocolate is the result of a complex, multi-stage process that has hardly changed in the past century. It begins on plantations nestled in equatorial jungles, but most of the profit is made by industrial factories in the global north. It isn't just the supply chain that remains unchanged. The power dynamics and economic inequalities of the chocolate industry are also holdovers from the colonial era.

DOWN ON THE FARM

The entire chocolate industry is rooted in cacao trees. Cacao trees are good producers, providing beans year-round with two main harvests. They are also very particular about their growing conditions, limited to warm, humid equatorial lowlands.

GROWING FORESTS OF FUTURE DELICIOUSNESS

Establishing a healthy and productive chocolate plantation is like starting a vineyard: it takes careful consideration and long-term planning. A grower has to consider soil and climate, select suitable trees, establish a canopy of taller shade trees to protect the cacao saplings, and cultivate layers of rotting leaves and empty pods on the ground as habitat for the midges that pollinate *Theobroma Cacao*.

In addition to its particular climate requirements, cacao is susceptible to a variety of diseases and pests. Fungal infections, hungry monkeys, and other factors can destroy over 40% of the crop in the eight months between flowering and harvest.

Different trees produce vastly different amounts and types of cacao. *Forastero*, the high-yield cacao that goes into 90% of all chocolate, can produce hundreds of football-sized pods. It lacks the depth of flavor, however, that is found in *Criollo* cacao, a favorite of the Aztecs that produces less than half as much fruit. Criollo is prized today by artisanal bean-to-bar manufacturers and companies like Valrhona and Amedi that cater to makers of fancy chocolate truffles. However, Criollo still only accounts for about 1% of the chocolate sold worldwide. The third and newest variety is *Trinitario*, a hardy hybrid that balances moderate yield with good flavor and goes into about 10% of chocolate.

Cacao pods are cut off the tree with a machete, drop to the ground, and are then harvested. For a few weeks after harvest they retain their brilliant colors and fruity pulp, but usually pods are opened almost immediately. Creo Chocolate works with farmers who open pods in the field and empty the pulp and beans into buckets so the pods can be left on the ground as midge habitat. Opening the pods has to be done carefully, because the beans themselves are delicate. A broken bean won't be protected by its shell from the bacteria that consume the pulp during fermentation, and could spoil the whole batch.

VIEWS OF A CACAO POD

CHOCOLATE'S CULINARY COUSIN
by Amy Bugbee

WHAT'S IN MY VANILLA?

"Natural Vanilla Flavor," "natural flavor," "and other natural flavors"—no doubt you have read these words on many a food label. Perhaps even on the ingredients label of a bottle claiming to be Pure Vanilla Extract. You may have even chosen this bottle of extract over the imitation stuff deeming it better. The truth is, neither Natural Vanilla Flavor nor imitation vanilla have anything to do with a vanilla bean!

"Natural Vanilla Flavor" can be any number of naturally occurring substances, according to the premier reference guide on the subject, a two thousand and some page book called *Fenaroli's Handbook of Flavor Ingredients*, by George A. Burdock. Commonly, "Natural Vanilla Flavor" is made from lignin, a tarry brown byproduct from wood processing, and waste product of paper mills. It is used for a variety of industrial and agricultural applications, including cement making, and in addition to Vanillin, it's used to make xylitol sugar!

Another substance used to create "Natural Vanilla Flavor" is castoreum, which is literally the castor sacs, or rather, glands from the nether regions of the furry, dam-building beaver,

VANILLA VINE AND CACAO TREE

FERMENTATION

The pods are discarded on site, and the beans and pulp are brought back from the field for fermentation. Small farms often ferment cacao in piles, covered with banana leaves. Larger operations often use wood or cement

boxes. Fermenting cacao is the first step in producing chocolate's complex flavor, and the chemistry of the fermentation process is as complex as the chocolate itself. The actual fermentation has little to do with cocoa beans, which are shielded from bacteria by their shells. The yeast and bacteria feed off the sugars in the white, gooey pulp, turning them into alcohols and acidic compounds. Some of these fermentation byproducts can pass through the shell into the bean, contributing to its bitter taste. Another factor in developing the bean's flavor is the heat generated by fermentation—usually around 130°F—which kills the bean and encourages enzymes that convert some of

which they use to mark their territory. Of course flavor and scent makers claim proprietary rights, and would never consider putting castoreum on the label—they are protected by the umbrella of "Natural Vanilla Flavor."

DIY VANILLA EXTRACT

The real mystery here is why? Sure, the vanilla bean is expensive and growing and curing it is a long and arduous process, but—and this is a big but, a huge but—the vanilla bean can be used over and over and over again! In fact, you can extract vanilla from vanilla beans until the bean disintegrates, and that takes years!

If you decide to make your own extract—to avoid the lignin and the castoreum, and who would blame you?—vanilla beans when treated properly in a mix of water and liquor can be used over and over again for years! And don't let that be their first stop, make it their last, after you've cooked with it, infused with it, and any other use you can think of, a simple rinse and dry, and your magical vanilla bean is ready to go again!

the bean's fat into sugars. Fermentation is one of the most important determinants of a bean's flavor.

Fermentation can take anywhere from three days to a full week. Too long, and the beans will rot. Too short, and they don't develop much flavor. That doesn't stop some growers from skipping

It's not entirely accurate to say that modern Criollo is the same cacao enjoyed by Aztec nobles. Plants hybridize and mutate, changing slightly with each generation. Chocolate maker Steve De Vries speaks in terms of Criollo-ness, evaluating cacao based on its similarity to a hypothetical ideal.

the step entirely, especially those that sell to industrial chocolate makers like Hershey and Nestlé, whose formulas are tailored to deliver consistent chocolate regardless of the beans' quality.

CACAO BEANS AND PULP IN A FERMENTATION BOX.

DRYING

Once fermented, cacao beans have to be dried so they won't rot during transport or storage. Sun-drying is favored for best flavor and is the simplest option for small-scale growers. It requires bringing the beans under cover at night, or any time it might rain, making it labor-intensive at larger scales. Heated air-dryers are more consistent than the sun, but exposure to smoke will alter the flavor of the beans, as will drying too fast.

Sun-drying can also have disadvantages for consumers. Kevin Straub of Creo Chocolate saw beans spread along Ecuadorean roadsides and sidewalks to dry, and Mort Rosenblum encountered the same thing in Africa. The beans get dry, but they might also get a light coating of motor oil. Even if the beans aren't dried on the road, animals may have access to the beans while they're drying as well, and can track feces onto them. For this reason, chocolate makers like Creo

Chocolate are strict about separating raw and roasted beans: roasting doubles as disinfection, and nobody wants to cross-contaminate.

Once the beans are dry, they can be shipped—under carefully controlled conditions, of course. Excess moisture will cause the beans to rot, and they can pick up scents and flavors from their surroundings. At least one chocolate maker has beans shipped in special bags implanted with tracking chips, so he can monitor them from his desk in Switzerland.

TIM, JANET, KEVIN, AND THE CHOCOLATE FACTORY

On entering the small Creo Chocolate factory in Portland, Oregon, the first thing you smell is chocolate, and the first thing you hear is a custom-built winnowing machine next to the door, just across from an elegant front counter where you can buy rich sipping chocolate and elegant bars that were produced in the very same room.

Janet and Tim Straub started Creo Chocolate with their son Kevin in 2014, but their story began years before, when the Straub family spent half a year touring the United States in an RV, visiting factories across the country to learn how things were made. That passion for creation and learning is what set them on the path to establishing their own educational factory. Today, Creo sells chocolate bars at several local shops in addition to their own storefront in the small central-city factory. Their passions are twofold: making good chocolate, and teaching people about it. That's why, several days a week, you can sign up for a class or free factory tour.

When we took the tour, Janet showed us a barrel of beans and pulp fresh from Ecuador so we could smell the acid-and-alcohol tang of fermenting cacao—something you normally find on the farm,

CHOCOLATE AS COMMODITY

Chocolate is many things to many people—comfort food, cash crop, confection—but to commodity brokers it's just another thing to trade.

Until the early 2000s, commodity traders in Chicago and New York relied on open outcry, shouting their orders across the floor of the exchange. Now they, like the London exchange, have gone electronic, with brokers sitting quietly at their desks and making trades via computer.

Commodity futures markets allow the industry to be more resilient in the face of bad growing seasons or wars like the recent ones in western Africa. The downside to the futures market is that speculators—like deep-pocketed hedge funds with no interest in the cacao itself—can cause unexpected price fluctuations that drive down the value of growers' beans while forcing chocolatiers to buy at high prices. The London market alone appears to trade 26 million tons of cacao every year, but it's really just the same three million tons of beans being swapped back and forth as the market fluctuates.

not in the factory. Our next stop was the roasting ovens, where beans go in on trays and come out darker, more flavorful, and ready to crack.

Much of Creo's technology is simple and/or DIY: the bean cracker, which splits the shell from the nib, is powered by a cordless drill. From there, the mixture of nibs and shells is carried up to a small custom-built winnower artfully placed in the window, where it blows the cacao through a a series of transparent tubes to separate out shell fragments and drops them into a bin in the basement—some local gardeners use them for mulch.

After a few minutes of shouting over the winnower's fan noise, we headed for a cramped back room to look at the refining and conching machines. When they started, the Straubs ran several of the little "Wonder Grinders" favored by home chocolatiers that can handle several-pound

batches. Since then, they've upgraded to bigger, higher-capacity machines that conch faster, and relegated the little grinders to making test batches. After about two days of conching, the chocolate is smooth and ready to be formed into large blocks that will age in cupboards behind the counter for at least a month.

Once aged, blocks of chocolate go to the tempering machine, which carefully heats, cools, and reheats them to establish the desired crystalline structure. Then, with the push of a button, molten chocolate pours from the nozzle into molds. The molds are hard plastic, sturdy enough to be slapped against the counter to eliminate air bubbles before they slide into the fridge to cool and harden.

Creo's process is the same one used by chocolate factories around the world for the past century, though each has their own minor variations. Valrhona, famous French maker of fine chocolate, operates ancient equipment in a sterile, climate-controlled environment to eliminate contaminants and produce chocolate that showcases the flavor of the bean without sacrificing consistency. Guittard Chocolate of San Francisco sometimes skips the molding and hardening steps, sending tanker trucks of liquid chocolate to the nearby See's Candy Factory, according to Elyce Zahn of nearby Cocotuttim chocolate.

Some of these factories are bean-to-bar companies like Creo, who source their cacao from specific growers, visiting Africa and South America to find top-notch beans and establish ties with farmers. Others, mostly larger companies like Valrhona and Felchin, focus on producing bulk chocolate that

> Samuel and Anna, the farmers that supply beans for Creo Chocolate, make test batches in their kitchen before shipping the beans. They roast beans in a clay pot on the stove, shell them by rolling the beans between their palms, and process them with a hand-cranked grinder. The result is coarse, but it's still chocolate!

they sell to bakers and chocolatiers instead of selling bars directly to consumers. Industrial chocolate makers may vertically integrate the process—from bean-buying stations in equatorial countries to globe-spanning production and sales operations—but they can't be as selective about their beans, and end up favoring consistency over quality.

EASY DIY CHOCOLATE MAKING

Making "real" chocolate bars at home isn't easy. Cocoa butter can be a challenging substance to work with — tempering takes patience and precision, and if you want to start from the bean itself, the processing steps are delicate and require specialized equipment.

We prefer to make chocolate the easy way: substitute coconut oil for cocoa butter. It's technically "compound chocolate," since it

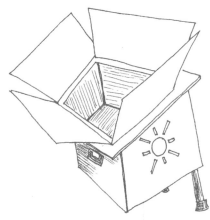

IF YOU WANT TO MELT COCONUT OIL (OR OTHER THINGS) WITH SOLAR POWER WHEN IT'S COLD OUT, TRY A SUN OVEN! IT'LL TAKE NO TIME AT ALL.

contains a fat other than cocoa butter. Many chocolatiers use the term with scorn because they see it as cheating the consumer out of the best possible product. We're not chocolatiers, though, and compound chocolate is both tasty and very easy to make.

When making chocolates in the winter, we use a simple double boiler to melt the coconut oil. To make the double boiler, fill a small pot or pan with water. Set a glass jar in the center, put the solid oil inside the jar, and bring the water to a boil. You can use a microwave or a stove on low heat as well, if you pay careful attention to make sure you don't start cooking it. If it's summer, leaving the coconut oil outside in the sun will also do the trick right quick.

Chocolate made this way doesn't have to be precise! Just taste-test the final mixture before pouring it into the mold. If you accidentally use more or less cocoa powder than the recipe calls for, your chocolate will probably still taste great. If you intentionally use way more or less sugar than the recipe calls for, you will make a deliciously sweet or bittersweet chocolate. If you mistakenly use way more fat than the recipe calls for, it's okay! Add more cocoa and sweetener to bring the flavor back to your chocolate bar. The following recipe is a good starting point for further experiments.

DARK CHOCOLATE: THE BASIC RECIPE

Our rule of thumb is that there should be equal amounts of cocoa powder and coconut oil. We use the next-smallest measuring cup for the sweetener. We prefer to make chocolate the easy way: substitute coconut oil for cocoa butter. It's technically "compound chocolate," since it contains a fat other than cocoa butter, but it's delicious and very easy to make.

1/3 cup cocoa powder (heaping)
1/3 cup melted coconut oil
1/4 cup powdered sugar or 3 tablespoons agave syrup

Many chocolatiers despise commercially-made compound chocolate because they see it as cheating the consumer out of the best possible product. For delicious homemade treats, though, it's hard to beat!

Combine the cocoa powder and the powdered sugar in a mixing bowl. Stir in the coconut oil. When the mixture is smooth, pour the mixture into a mold.

Leave it in the freezer for 10 to 20 minutes; larger bars will take longer to cool. Store this chocolate in a cool place, ideally the fridge or freezer, until ready to eat. If you need to transport it—especially if the weather is warm—leave it in the freezer for a while and take it out immediately before you leave.

After you have tried the basic recipe, we encourage experimentation! The consistency of your chocolate mix can vary wildly. There are recipes out there

AGAVE SYRUP IS A GOOD ALTERNATIVE TO POWDERED SUGAR FOR CHOCOLATE BARS

for chocolate that contain very small quantities of sweetener, and those that contain next to no cocoa powder. As long as you come up with something that tastes good to you, go ahead and throw it in the mold. It will usually come out chocolate and merriment.

If you want to try a different blend of flavors, pair or replace the cocoa with other bitter and savory powders. Here are a few suggestions.

COFFEE BAR: Instant coffee will make a coffee bar. You may find fairtrade instant coffee in a few grocery stores, or look online. Decaf is also an option, or try powdered coffee replacements such as the Polish roasted grain beverage "Inka."

CAROB BAR: Carob powder gives a flavor very similar to chocolate but is slightly sweeter.

SOUR CANDY: Replace the cocoa powder with a brightly-colored sports drink powder.

MOLDS

You can use all sorts of things as chocolate molds. Here are a few of our favorites:

Mini-cupcake cups
Parchment paper
Silicone molds
Thin-walled plastic
containers (greased)
Waxed paper

Silicone molds are great for making chocolate. They don't require greasing, they can make simple or detailed chocolates, and it's easy to pop out the chocolates after they have hardened. The best silicone mold that we have found to date is the meatloaf mold. We pour a shallow layer of chocolate in the bottom. This yields a large rectangular bar of chocolate. We also enjoy the widely-available silicone trays with heart-shaped indentations, which make quintessential chocolate treats.

Mini-cupcake cups are great for party chocolates. There are two ways to use them. You can pour chocolate directly into the cups, or pre-make individual chocolates and then move them to the cups. In a pinch, you can also use any thin-walled plastic container as a mold. Grease lightly using vegetable oil that is liquid at room temperature.

Another alternative is to use parchment paper or waxed paper. These are great for making a chocolate bark. To contain the chocolate, you can set the paper on a large plate or put it in a baking tray.

FRUIT AND NUT CHOCOLATE BAR

1/3 cup cocoa powder (heaping)
1/3 cup coconut oil
1/4 cup powdered sugar
1/3–1/2 cup trail mix

Combine the cocoa powder and the powdered sugar in a mixing bowl. If your coconut oil isn't already a liquid, take care of that now. Stir in the coconut oil. Add trail mix. Pour the mixture into a mold. This will make a standard chunky chocolate bar.

To make fruit & nut chocolate clusters, increase the amount to a cup of trail mix and dip out spoonfuls onto wax paper. It will hold together better if you allow it to cool slightly before spooning it out.

Here are some alternative ingredients to go in or on your chunky chocolate bars. Mix and match as appropriate:

Banana chips (sweet or salty)
Coarse salt
Fruits (dried/freeze-dried)
Nuts & Seeds (chopped)
Puffed rice
Toasted coconut
Toasted oats
Wasabi peanuts
Candied flowers
Candied ginger
Candied nuts (page 167)
Candy cane (blended)

Melt coconut oil using a double boiler or solar oven. If you're careful not to overheat the oil, you can also melt it directly on the stove or in the microwave.

Cereals, especially those marketed toward children
Chips (e.g., barbecue)Pop rocks
Pretzel pieces
Cocoa nibs. Mark the chocolates with decaf differently from those with coffee beans!

PARTY BITES

Use techniques from the *Dark Chocolate* (page 160) and *Chunky Chocolate* (page 163) recipes to make these favorite flavor combinations. We recommend making at least a double batch for social gatherings.

ORANGE CARROT GINGER: Follow the chunky recipe using candied ginger and shredded carrots. Add orange essential oil.

ROCKY ROAD: Follow the chunky recipe using chopped almonds and chopped marshmallows. Add vanilla essential oil.

REVERSE S'MORE: Follow the chunky recipe using broken fragments of graham crackers and chopped marshmallows.

NESTED S'MORES: Follow the recipe for reverse s'mores. Place the resulting chocolate in a graham cracker sandwich along with a marshmallow. Then, following the dip 'n drizzle recipe, coat the sandwich with reverse s'mores. Repeat.

SALTED ALMOND-HAZELNUT: Follow the chunky recipe using chopped almonds and hazelnuts. Add almond and hazelnut essential oils. Sprinkle coarse salt onto the top of the chocolate bar before refrigeration.

TOMATO-BASIL: Follow the chunky recipe using diced sundried tomatoes. If the tomatoes are dried, infuse basil in olive oil and add up to a tablespoon of the infusion. If the tomatoes are packed in oil, omit this step.

DIP AND DRIZZLE

When the basic recipe is warm enough, it can be used for dipping and coating other foods.

Bite-sized fruits and other foodstuffs can be placed on a tray of waxed paper and then drizzled with chocolate. Alternately, add a cup's worth to the basic recipe and ladle out the resulting mixture either into molds or onto waxed paper. Most larger fruits will do best sliced. Bananas, bread, and carrots can be dipped whole or when sliced/cubed, and then placed on a tray for refrigeration.

The Fruit and Nut Chocolate Bar recipe (page 163) is also a great place to look for ingredients that can be dipped and drizzled upon. You can also use flavored, spiced, or infused chocolates for combinations like mint-blueberry or ginger-orange-cinnamon.

Bananas
Blackberries
Blueberries
Chili peppers (seeded)
Dried fruits
Figs
Kiwis
Peaches
Pears
Raisins
Strawberries
Cherries. If you pit the cherry, you lose the stem. If you don't pit the cherry, it is best to warn people.

Biscotti
Bread
Candied ginger
Popsicles
Pretzels
Some bugs (not vegan)
Sweet carrots
That which grows in your garden
Zucchini
Chocolate chip cookie dough balls

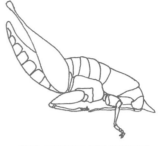

YES, CHOCOLATE-COATED
GRASSHOPPERS ARE A THING!

Almonds
Brazil Nuts
Cashews
Filberts
Flax seeds (use sparingly)
Pecans
Peanuts
Pepitas
Sunflower seeds
Walnuts
Peanut butter filled pretzels. Buy these pre-made, squish peanut butter into pretzels, or use the filling from the peanut butter cup recipe.
Honeycomb candy (page 168)

★ ★ ★ ★ ★  ★ ★ ★ ★ ★

CANDIED NUTS

This recipe is excellent for coating in chocolate.

1/4 cup sugar
1/4 teaspoon salt
1 tablespoon honey
1 tablespoon water
2 cups nuts

Cover a large plate or cookie sheet with parchment paper, waxed paper, or greased foil. If you need a hard glaze, preheat the oven to 425°F.

Mix all ingredients except the nuts in a heavy pan on medium-high heat and stir occasionally for 3 to 4 minutes, until the sugar dissolves completely and turns golden. Add the nuts and reduce the heat to medium-low, and keep stirring the mixture for another two minutes, until it turns golden-brown.

If you want the harder glaze, put the pan in your preheated oven. Stir after five minutes and put back in for another 5-10 minutes, keeping a close eye on them to catch the bright, shiny glaze. They burn easily if left too long.

Spread the candied nuts on the baking sheet to cool for ten minutes or so before breaking them into chunks. These chunks can now be used in chocolate recipes. Yields enough candied nuts for 2 batches of *Fruit and Nut Chocolate Bars* (page 163).

HONEYCOMB CANDY

1/3 cup butter
1/3 cup corn syrup
2/3 cup sugar
3 tablespoon water
2 1/2 tablespoons baking soda
2 batches of dark chocolate
(page 160)

Line an 8 x 8-inch glass or metal baking dish with parchment paper, waxed paper, or greased foil.

Sift the baking soda and measure out a level tablespoon. In a large saucepan over medium heat combine everything except the baking soda and chocolate, and stir continuously. It's important for the saucepan to be much larger than the volume of the mixture, because adding baking soda will cause it to grow substantially.

Once the sugar is completely dissolved, increase the heat to medium-high and stop stirring. Let the mixture boil for about five minutes. If you have a candy thermometer, use it to check the temperature.

Keep a close eye on it for the moment when it turns golden-brown or caramel-colored. The thermometer will read 280°F, which is known among candy makers as "hard crack." If you need to confirm this without a thermometer, take your saucepan off the heat for a moment, dip the handle of a metal spoon in it, and then dip it into a cup of cold water. The candy may audibly crack as it hardens. If it doesn't, pull the spoon out of the water and bite the candy coating off the end of the spoon. If it breaks off and leaves the spoon clean, you're set. If not, return the sugar mixture to the heat briefly.

When the mixture reaches hard crack, pull it off the heat, mix in the baking soda, and watch your honeycomb expand!

Drop the mixture into the lined baking dish and let cool for at least 30 minutes without touching or jostling it. Once it has cooled completely, break it into chunks with a knife and dip in chocolate as you would anything else. Yields enough honeycomb for 2 batches of dark chocolate. Remember to floss after eating.

Chocolate made this way doesn't have to be precise! Just taste-test the final mixture before pouring it into the mold. If you accidentally use more or less cocoa powder than the recipe calls for, your chocolate will probably still taste great. If you intentionally use way more or less sugar than the recipe calls for, you will make a deliciously sweet or bittersweet chocolate. If you mistakenly use way more fat than the recipe calls for, it's okay! Add more cocoa and sweetener to bring the flavor back to your chocolate bar.

Our rule of thumb is that there should be equal amounts of cocoa powder and coconut oil. We use the next-smallest measuring cup for the sweetener.

THE
SCIENCE
OF
CHOCOLATE

"More than 100 medicinal uses for cocoa were described in manuscripts produced between the 16th and 20th century." (*Chocolate and Health*)

I f you're looking for a wide-eyed, uncritical puff piece on chocolate's potential health benefits, look elsewhere. We recognize that cacao could be beneficial in many ways—in addition to being delicious. But we also know that chocolate won't cure everything that might ail you. Its effect on the human body is extremely complicated, and nobody fully understands it yet.

Reporting on nutritional research often glosses over details like small sample sizes and conflicting results. I've read breathless news articles based on studies with only ten subjects, and seen reporters ignore the fact that the drug being tested sometimes isn't even chocolate, it's concentrated cacao extract so bitter most people refuse to eat it.

It's also worth remembering that many studies are funded by companies that benefit from particular results. Hershey and Mars are the biggest players in this arena, but the same goes for smaller companies like UK-based InFirst, which is developing the theobromine-based cough medicine mentioned below. Even if sponsors don't affect the conclusions, they can determine what research is funded. That means we're far more likely to see studies on the positive side of chocolate than the negative side.

In the following chapter, we'll take a systematic look at what is known about chocolate's medicinal and nutritional value. To start with, we'll run

A CACAO POD, FILLED WITH DOZENS OF ALMOND-SIZED BEANS

through some of the notable chemical compounds found in cacao, and what effect they have on the human body. With that as a foundation, we can discuss chocolate's nutritional value and the effects it can have on human health—from the definite to the improbable.

FLAVONOIDS: CHOCOLATE AND THE HEART

Throughout history, chocolate has been touted as an aphrodisiac, a "pure food," and a magical panacea. Today, when people talk about the health benefits of chocolate, they're most often referring to recent research on flavonoids.

There is some good evidence that flavonoids from chocolate may have beneficial effects on cardiovascular health, but it's far from certain. The study that started research in that direction has recently been called into question, and the mechanisms by which cacao affects the human circulatory system are poorly understood.

Researchers were inspired to investigate the effect of chocolate on heart health when a study of the Kuna—people indigenous to South America who tend to eat large quantities of chocolate—revealed that they had an extremely low risk of cardiovascular disease. The exception to this rule was those Kuna who went to live in urban areas, and as a result consumed less cacao.

Since the initial Kuna findings, numerous studies have taken different approaches to verifying cacao's effect on the heart and circulatory system. One found that older people with mild hypertension had lower blood pressure after 18 weeks of eating about 6 grams of dark chocolate per day. Another study evaluated nearly five thousand people in the US and found an "inverse correlation between chocolate consumption and the prevalence of cardiovascular disease." Other

studies in Germany and Sweden have had similar results. It seems fairly clear that eating a little cacao probably reduces high blood pressure and risk of stroke.

The reason for this probably has something to do with flavonoids' antioxidant effect. Plant-derived antioxidants are often credited with miraculous healing powers, from curing cancer to reversing aging, because they can prevent certain types of cell damage. The flavonoids in cacao, however, don't make it to most of the body. The only places they reach in any substantial concentration are the bloodstream and the gastrointestinal tract. So it's unlikely that cacao flavonoids will reach skin,

FLAVONOIDS AND PHENOLS AND CATECHINS, OH MY!

For this chapter, I'll mostly stick to the term *"flavonoids."* If you're reading about chocolate elsewhere, though, the language can get complex.

When we talk about flavonoids in chocolate, we're usually talking about *catechin* and *epicatechin*. (Some authors don't mention epicatechin, since the two are isomers—they have the same atoms, just arranged differently.) Catechin and epicatechin are *flavanols*, which is a subcategory of flavonoids. Because flavonoids have multiple phenol groups, they are sometimes called by the even broader term *polyphenols*.

You may also encounter the word "antioxidant," which is very general in a different way. All the previous terms describe chemical formulas and structures, but "antioxidant" refers to how a compound behaves in certain chemical reactions. Some antioxidants are flavonoids, but not all flavonoids are antioxidants.

bones, or lungs, but they might actually have an impact on your blood and your heart—and at least one study confirms that within two hours of consuming 45 grams of dark chocolate, your blood cells are more resistant to oxidative damage than than they are after you eat flavonoid-free white chocolate.

Researchers have explored cacao flavonoids' effect on all sorts of other things: skin health, cognitive function, insulin sensitivity, and cholesterol levels are among the more notable. It's too soon to draw any conclusions, though, since most of those are exploratory studies. Moreover, some of the studies aren't even using chocolate. They actually perform the tests with cacao extract, a concentrated flavonoid powder so bitter many people refuse to eat it.

Studies of cocoa flavonoids still refer back to the original Kuna findings as the first evidence that cacao reduces blood pressure. But in 2013, cultural geographer Jeffrey Barnes questioned that research. In visits to Panama, he noticed that the Kuna ate less chocolate than originally reported. Furthermore, they rarely consumed locally-grown cacao, preferring imported Colombian cacao that was lower in flavonoids. Whatever it is that keeps the Kuna in excellent cardiovascular health, there's a good chance it has nothing to do with their cacao intake.

NUTRIENTS AND ANTINUTRIENTS

Cacao is full of trace minerals and other nutrients. The exact mix varies depending on growing conditions, fermentation, and even grinding machinery. Unfortunately, cacao also contains numerous

antinutrients: compounds that reduce our bodies' ability to absorb things like iron and calcium from food.

On the one hand, chocolate contains copper, iron, magnesium, calcium, potassium, and zinc—all crucial, in small quantities, for our bodies. Some of those minerals come from the soil, but others may be deposited in chocolate by grinding machinery.

On the other hand, chocolate is high in antinutrients like flavonoids (yes, the very same beneficial chemicals from the previous section) and organic acids, which both reduce nutrient absorption. As a result, it's hard to tell what nutrients you're really getting from chocolate.

Iron is a good example of this complexity. The iron in chocolate is more concentrated than chicken liver or beef. Unfortunately, chocolate—like all plants—contains mostly non-heme iron, which is less bioavailable than the heme iron in meat. So there's plenty of iron in chocolate, but not all of it makes its way into your body. In addition, flavonoids and some organic acids can block iron absorption, so you'll get even less iron from raw cacao or lightly-roasted chocolate. If you want to absorb chocolate's iron content, eat it with foods that are high in Vitamin C, such as citrus.

Given the variability of cacao sourcing and processing, it's very difficult to say for sure what nutrients you'll ultimately get out of a given bean, let alone how your body will handle them.

BIOGENIC AMINES

Literally, these are "amines produced by living organisms or biological processes," and they show up all over the place in biological systems. In the human body, various biogenic amines serve as neurotransmitters

regulating everything from sleep and appetite to motivation and addiction.

Some of the biogenic amines present in chocolate affect the vascular system, causing symptoms like blushing and blood pressure variations. It's possible for their effects to be more severe, though, ranging from headaches to potentially fatal cardiovascular shock. Fortunately, the quantity of biogenic amines in chocolate is small, though it may increase slightly with extra roasting.

Perhaps the best-documented single biogenic amine in chocolate is phenylethylamine, which triggers the release of dopamine and noradrenaline in humans. Some people think it is responsible for chocolate's aphrodisiac effect, because dopamine is associated with infatuation and love. Others claim it may delay fatigue and increase stamina—something people have believed about chocolate since the early colonial era, if not before.

Some chocolate experts, however, argue that the amount of phenylethylamine in cacao is so minuscule that its effect on neurochemistry is negligible. So far, there doesn't seem to be enough evidence to definitively sway the argument in either direction, and it's complicated by the differences between individuals and the brain's ability to acclimate to stimuli.

Another biogenic amine that could be responsible for the joy people derive from chocolate is anandamide. That's because it is a cannabinoid compound; it activates the same receptors in the human nervous system as the THC in cannabis. It's unlikely you'll get high off chocolate, though—like phenylethylamine, anandamide shows up in chocolate in very low concentrations. If you try to reach an altered state

of consciousness by eating cacao, you'll probably only be conscious of a full stomach.

THEOBROMINE AND FRIENDS

Theobromine is to chocolate as caffeine is to coffee. Both, plus the theophylline in tea, are notable stimulants from the same chemical family, the methylxanthines. They have many effects on humans, but they're best known for suppressing drowsiness—as anyone who has had a shot of espresso in the evening will know.

Theobromine is a key part of chocolate's molecular signature, occurring in only a handful of plants (tea, yerba mate, kola nuts, and a few others). Cacao also contains caffeine, so archaeologists look for the two together when identifying ancient Mesoamerican pottery that may have contained chocolate. Theophylline (the characteristic methylxanthine in tea) is present in cacao as well, though its concentration depends on the variety.

All methylxanthines are stimulants, but they may have slightly different effects. Caffeine, especially in large doses, tends to leave you wired and jittery. Theobromine has a weaker effect on the nervous system. It lowers blood pressure, which may be why chocolate is known for inducing general happiness. Theobromine's stimulant effects may also be partially responsible for chocolate's reputation as an aphrodisiac. Theophylline—present in cacao, but more often associated with tea—tends to increase blood pressure, and eases

A THEOBROMINE MOLECULE

breathing. While even the amount of theophylline in a cup of tea is too small to have a noticeable effect, in higher concentrations it is used to treat asthma and other respiratory diseases.

In addition to its role as a stimulant, theobromine has an effect on the respiratory system similar to that of theophylline. It has recently been tested as a cough suppressant, though theobromine-based cough medication isn't yet available in most of the world. An initial trial suggested theobromine may actually be better than codeine as a cough suppressant, but there were only ten test subjects. The dose tested was around 1000mg, which you can get from as little as fifty grams (two ounces) of dark chocolate, depending on how it is processed and prepared. Full-scale clinical trials have been completed in both South Korea and the UK, but the results are not yet available. In early 2016 we checked with the lead researcher, Professor Alyn Morice, who said they are waiting to publish until the medication is ready to go before regulatory bodies.

Theobromine has one other notable effect: given a high enough dose, it is poisonous. While it's usually very difficult to get a lethal dose from eating chocolate, people with certain genetic conditions may be far more susceptible. Other animals are much more susceptible to the effects of theobromine. It's been used to poison coyotes and dope racehorses. It definitely affects dogs, cats, birds, pigs, and cows. Plenty of people have a dog who has gorged themselves on Hershey's Kisses, but it doesn't mean the dog is immune. It's actually a reflection of the low cacao content in commercial milk chocolates. That same dog could be in serious trouble if they get their paws on a bar of 70% dark. Initial symptoms of theobromine poisoning include nausea and

vomiting, as well as diarrhea, but severe cases can lead to seizures and heart attacks.

THEOBROMINE POISONING DOSAGES

	Dose that would kill 50% of dogs (LD_{50})	Lowest dose known to have a toxic effect on humans (TD_{Lo})	Daily dose that is known to have a substantial negative effect on humans
Pure Theobromine	0.005 oz/lb	0.0004 oz/lb	0.016 oz/lb
Raw Cacao	0.16–0.32 oz/lb	.01-.02 oz/lb	0.5–1 oz/lb
Dark Chocolate	1 oz/lb	.09 oz/lb	3.5 oz/lb
Milk Chocolate	3 oz/lb	0.27 oz/lb	10 oz/lb

Based on these dosages some simple math tells us how much chocolate you (or your dog) would have to eat to be affected. Dosages are described by the quantity of poison per pound of body weight. Given, for example, the dose of dark chocolate needed to have a substantial effect on most people (3.5 ounces per pound) we can multiply by the weight of the average human (137 pounds) to determine that they would have to eat 29.8 pounds of dark chocolate, on a daily basis, to meet that level. Someone with a low tolerance for theobromine, however, could experience some effects after consuming only 12 ounces of dark chocolate—several large bars. It takes even less raw cacao to have the same effect. Milk chocolate's theobromine content is about one third that of dark chocolate, so it takes far more to have a comparable effect.

CHOCOLATE HEADACHES
Enough people report chocolate headaches and migraines that several epidemiological studies have been conducted, and cacao usually

comes in fairly high on the list, following only stress, inconsistent sleep, menstruation, alcohol, and hunger.

That may sound like pretty clear evidence, but remember that epidemiological studies are usually just surveys; all it means is that if you ask people, lots of them will say chocolate causes their migraines or other headaches. When you get into the lab, the story changes. Double-blind studies, with control groups receiving a carob-based placebo instead of chocolate, reached very different conclusions. In those, participants who ate the placebo were just as likely to get headaches as those who ate real chocolate.

Why the discrepancy? It could have to do with the size of the studies. Even the largest double-blind study of headache triggers had only 67 participants. They may, through sheer bad luck, have gotten a disproportionately low percentage of people whose migraines are triggered by cacao. That theory is supported by some older, even smaller studies that only involved people who had already identified chocolate as a potential migraine trigger—they found a strong positive correlation between chocolate and headaches. So it's possible that the larger studies weren't really big enough to accurately represent the entire population.

On the other hand, it's possible the double-blind studies are correct, and chocolate is not a trigger for most migraine sufferers. In that case, there would be a couple of possible explanations for the high number of people who still report that chocolate causes their migraines.

One theory is that chocolate seems like a migraine trigger because common migraine triggers also cause chocolate cravings. Stress and hunger can both encourage people to eat chocolate, and

they're also among the most common and well-verified migraine triggers. It's possible a migraine sufferer might eat chocolate when stressed, tired, or hungry, and later get a migraine for the same reason.

The other possibility is that for some people, chocolate might be only part of the headache trigger. Chocolate alone is fine, but it could cause trouble when combined with other factors like stress or sleeplessness. This seems plausible, given the effects of the chemicals in chocolate. Theobromine and biogenic amines affect the nervous system. They also, like flavonoids, have an effect on blood pressure and heart rate. Since migraine headaches result from both neurological and vascular factors, it wouldn't be surprising if chocolate contributes to migraines, even if it doesn't cause them on its own.

CHOCOLATE AND MOOD

Depending on who you ask, you might hear that "Chocolate appears to promote the neurotransmitter serotonin release as well, thereby producing calming, pleasurable feelings" (*Chocolate as Medicine*).

Hernando Cortés, the Spaniard who took control of the Aztec empire, also noticed its stimulating effect, saying that "A cup of this precious drink permits a man to walk for a whole day without food."

The general sense of positivity might come from biogenic amines like phenylethylamine or the cannabinoid anandamide, while theobromine is almost certainly the stimulant. There's probably also a psychological component. Chocolate is associated with holidays and special events, love and happiness. Those associations inform the feelings we experience when we eat chocolate, in addition to whatever chemical effect it has.

If you want to improve your mood with chocolate, you should know that the effect probably won't last. At least one researcher has found that while people enjoy anticipating and eating chocolate, that pleasure doesn't negate depression and it is often followed by guilt.

CHOCOLATE AND LAXATIVES

Apart from claims about the health value of cacao itself, chocolate has long been used as a flavoring for unpalatable medicines and vitamins.

One of those chocolate-flavored medicines is Ex-Lax. The active ingredient is senna, which is quite bitter, but sweetened chocolate helps it taste better. The only problem with chocolate-flavored laxatives is that people occasionally enjoy them a bit too much, and overdose on the potent laxative hidden under the tasty chocolate.

Recent research, however, indicates that chocolate may affect the gastrointestinal system in its own right. Cacao extract inhibits the

activity of *Escherichia coli* and *Vibro cholera* in the intestine. This would corroborate the traditional Mesoamerican use of cacao to treat diarrhea.

"HEALTHY" CHOCOLATE

Not all chocolate is created equal, and the kind that's cheapest and easiest to get—sweet, highly processed bars—is the least likely to be beneficial.

The best option is plain cacao, either beans or nibs. The concentration of flavonoids, which seem to be generally beneficial, decreases with fermentation and roasting, so the closer you get to raw cacao, the better off you are. Flavonoids, in addition to promoting cardiovascular health, are very bitter, so you can use bitterness as a quick-and-dirty test for healthy cacao beans. It doesn't work so well on sweetened chocolate, though, unless you know

ON "SUPERFOODS"

In recent years, the food industry has latched onto the term "superfood"—applying it to anything deemed nutritious, especially fruits and vegetables that are high in antioxidants. The chocolate industry has leapt onto the bandwagon, which isn't entirely surprising. Throughout its history the fruit of the cacao tree has been hailed as magical and medicinal. While recent nutritional studies support the notion that chocolate may have beneficial effects as one component of a well-balanced diet, there's little basis for some of the medical miracles attributed to it.

"Superfood," like so many food labels ("natural" and "pure" come to mind) is a marketing term and nothing more. It has no regulated meaning or standard definition. Its purpose, as Tom Philpott, writing for Mother Jones Magazine, points out, is not to inform but to sell products. "People can only eat so much, and in industrialized countries where food is plentiful, they don't tend to consume more

> of it as their incomes grow. . . . One way the industry responds to this stagnation is to roll out 'new and improved' products." In some cases, those "new and improved" foods are the same old thing in fresh packaging, and that's generally the case with "superfood" chocolate.

that the varieties you're comparing have identical amounts of sugar.

If you get your chocolate in bars, you'll want the maximum cocoa content. According to *Chocolate and Health*, "From experience, a dark chocolate containing about 2% flavanols [a subcategory of flavonoids] is really on the edge of being too bitter. Currently 70% cocoa chocolates only contain about 0.7% of flavanols because of heavy processing. The same chocolate would still be tasty with the flavanols content at least double." This means that darker chocolates are often best. You can also look for makers that specify low roasting temperatures.

Because flavonoids are heat sensitive, their concentration changes when you cook or bake chocolate. There are a few tricks to maximize flavonoid content when cooking besides just keeping the temperature low. Cacao flavonoids survive best when cooked with minimal water and plenty of fat in high-density foods. For example, if you make a chocolate cake with cocoa powder, it will lose more flavonoids than the same cake made with baking chocolate, which contains more fat. A dense brownie is preferable to a light, fluffy one.

If you're cooking with cocoa powder, check whether it has been alkalized or "dutched." This process was developed to help it dissolve better in water instead of clumping, but it can reduce the flavonoid content by over seventy percent. Alkalization may also affect the bioavailability of the flavanols that remain.

Special thanks to Joshua K. Endow, plant biologist, for reviewing this chapter!

BIBLIOGRAPHY

RECIPE AND COOKING

"5 Sweet and Savory Things to Do With Cocoa Nibs." *Food52*. Accessed August 6, 2015. http://food52.com/blog/9783-5-sweet-and-savory-things-to-do-with-cocoa-nibs.

Alford, Jeffrey, and Naomi Duguid. *Seductions of Rice: A Cookbook*. New York: Artisan, 1998.

Batra, Neelam. *Chilis to Chutneys: American Home Cooking with the Flavors of India*. 1st ed. New York: William Morrow, 1998.

Bittman, Mark. *How to Cook Everything Vegetarian: Simple Meatless Recipes for Great Food*. Hoboken, NJ: Wiley, 2007.

Brill, Steve. *The Wild Vegan Cookbook: A Forager's Culinary Guide (in the Field or in the Supermarket) to Preparing and Savoring Wild (and Not so Wild) Natural Foods*. Pbk. ed. Boston, Mass: The Harvard Common Press, 2010.

Bull, Lorena Novak. *The Everything Vegan Baking Cookbook*. An Everything Series Book. Avon, Mass: Adams Media, 2012.

"Champorado Recipe." *ASTIG Vegan*. Accessed August 14, 2015. http://www.astigvegan.com/champorado-recipe/.

"Chocolate Oblivion Truffle Torte." *101 Cookbooks*. Accessed August 20, 2015. http://www.101cookbooks.com/archives/000287.html.

"Chocolate: Or, An Indian Drinke, by Antonio Colmenero." Accessed April 26, 2016. https://www.gutenberg.org/files/21271/21271-h/21271-h.htm.

Christensen, Emma. "What's the Difference? Brown, Green, and Red Lentils." *The Kitchn*, March 15, 2010. http://www.thekitchn.com/whats-the-difference-brown-gre-111139.

"Cinnamon and Cayenne and Chocolate, Oh My!" Accessed October 6, 2015. http://ask.metafilter.com/286709/Cinnamon-and-Cayenne-and-Chocolate-Oh-My.

Clark, Melissa. "Roasted Beets With Chiles, Ginger, Yogurt and Indian Spices Recipe - NYT Cooking." Accessed July 13, 2015. http://cooking.nytimes.com/recipes/1013864-roasted-beets-with-chiles-ginger-yogurt-and-indian-spices.

"Facebook Group: Vegan Meringue - Hits and Misses!" *Vegan Meringue - Hits and Misses!* Accessed June 14, 2016. https://www.facebook.com/groups/VeganMeringue/.

Fenaroli, Giovanni. *Fenaroli's Handbook of Flavor Ingredients: Adapted from the Italian Language Works of Giovanni Fenaroli*. 2d ed. Cleveland: CRC Press, 1975.

"Homemade Vegan Pizza." *No Meat Athlete*. Accessed August 13, 2015. http://www.nomeatathlete.com/vegan-pizza-recipe/.

"How to Cook Green or Brown Lentils." *wikiHow*. Accessed May 8, 2016. http://www.wikihow.com/Cook-Green-or-Brown-Lentils.

Laudan, Rachel. "The Technical Bases of Mole and Curry." *Rachel Laudan*, September 27, 2008. http://www.rachellaudan.com/2008/09/the-technical-bases-of-mole-and-curry.html.

Makris, Dimetra. *Delicious Quick Breads and Muffins*. 1st ed. New York: Fawcett Columbine, 1987.

McFadden, Christine, and Christine France. *The Cook's Guide to Chocolate*. London: Hermes House, 2000.

Nakos, Debby Maugans. *Small-Batch Baking for Chocolate Lovers*. New York: St. Martin's Griffin, 2011.

Ostmann, Barbara Gibbs, and Jane L. Baker. *The Recipe Writer's Handbook*. New York: Wiley, 1997.

Page, Karen, and Andrew Dornenburg. *The Flavor Bible: The Essential Guide to Culinary Creativity, Based on the Wisdom of America's Most Imaginative Chefs*. 1st ed. New York: Little, Brown and Company, 2008.

"Pozole - Wikipedia, the Free Encyclopedia." Accessed June 18, 2016. https://en.wikipedia.org/wiki/Pozole.

Robertson, Robin. *1,000 Vegan Recipes*. Hoboken, N.J: John Wiley & Sons, 2009.

Snyder, Amy R., and Justin Snyder. *The Everything Vegan Slow Cooker Cookbook*. Avon, Massachusetts: Adams Media, 2012.

Spieler, Marlena. "Chickpeas With Thai Chilies Recipe - NYT Cooking." Accessed July 13, 2015. http://cooking.nytimes.com/recipes/9373-chickpeas-with-thai-chilies.

"Vegan Zucchini Brownies." Accessed August 3, 2015. http://theliveinkitchen.com/2014/07/21/vegan-zucchini-brownies/.

Velden, Dana. "How To Chop, Dice, and Mince an Onion — Cooking Lessons from The Kitchn." *The Kitchn*, April 26, 2013. http://www.thekitchn.com/how-to-understand-mince-chop-and-dice-cooking-lessons-from-the-kitchn-188523.

Vijayakar, Sunil, and Pilar Guerrero. *200 recetas económicas*, 2011.

Vollstedt, Maryana. *The Big Book of Breakfast: Serious Comfort Food for Any Time of the Day*. San Francisco: Chronicle Books, 2003.

Waters, Alice, Kelsie Kerr, and Patricia Curtan. *The Art of Simple Food II: Recipes, Flavor, and Inspiration from the New Kitchen Garden*. First edition. New York: Clarkson Potter/Publishers, 2013.

Wells, Troth. *The World in Your Kitchen*. London: New Internationalist Publications, 1995.

Whitman, Joan, and Dolores Simon. *Recipes into Type: A Handbook for Cookbook Writers and Editors*. 1st ed. New York: HarperCollins, 1993.

Zachos, Ellen. *Backyard Foraging: 65 Familiar Plants You Didn't Know You Could Eat*. North Adams, MA: Storey Publishing, 2013.

Okakura Kakuzō. *The Book of Tea*. Tokyo; New York: Kodansha International, 2005.

HISTORY, PRODUCTION, AND SCIENCE OF CHOCOLATE BIBLIOGRAPHY

"A Double-Blind Provocative Study Chocolate as a Trigger of Headache." Accessed April 8, 2016. http://www.thomaswalser.ch/ceph_marcus_1997.pdf.

Adams, Stephen. "'Chocolate Cure' for Persistent Cough," December 20, 2010. http://www.telegraph.co.uk/news/health/news/8214459/Chocolate-cure-for-persistent-cough.html.

"Are Quinoa, Chia Seeds, and Other 'Superfoods' a Scam?" *Mother Jones*. Accessed March 14, 2016. http://www.motherjones.com/environment/2013/05/are-superfoods-quinoa-chia-goji-good-for-you.

"Bean To Bar | Guittard." Accessed March 14, 2016. https://www.guittard.com/bean-to-bar.

"Bloody Valentine: Child Slavery in Ivory Coast's Cocoa Fields." *Mother Jones*. Accessed March 14, 2016. http://www.motherjones.com/tom-philpott/2012/02/ivory-coast-cocoa-chocolate-child-slavery.

"Can the Chocolate Industry Change Its Ways?" Accessed March 14, 2016. http://thecnnfreedomproject.blogs.cnn.com/2014/03/06/can-the-chocolate-industry-change-its-ways/.

Cherny, Andrei. *The Candy Bombers: The Untold Story of the Berlin Airlift and America's Finest Hour*. New York: G.P. Putnam's Sons, 2008.

"Chiles, Chocolate, and Race in New Spain: Glancing Backward to Spain or Looking Forward to Mexico?" Accessed March 24, 2016. http://www.rachellaudan.com/wp-content/uploads/2007/08/Chiles-Chocolate-and-Race.pdf.

"Chocolate and Slavery." *1843*, December 29, 2013. https://www.1843magazine.com/places/chocolate-and-slavery.

"Chocolate Health Benefits Traced to Panamanian Tribe Get 2nd Look." Accessed March 14, 2016. http://www.cbc.ca/news/health/chocolate-s-health-touters-may-have-misunderstood-local-reality-of-tribe-1.2883561.

"Chocolate: Or, An Indian Drinke, by Antonio Colmenero." Accessed April 26, 2016. https://www.gutenberg.org/files/21271/21271-h/21271-h.htm.

CNN, By Matt Percival. "From Bean to Bar: Why Chocolate Will Never Taste the Same Again." *CNN*. Accessed March 14, 2016. http://www.cnn.com/2014/02/13/world/africa/cocoa-nomics-from-bean-to-bar/index.html.

"Cocoa Extract - Scientific Review on Usage, Dosage, Side Effects." *Examine.com*. Accessed March 14, 2016. https://examine.com/supplements/cocoa-extract/.

"Cocoa-Nomics Explained: Unwrapping the Chocolate Industry." Accessed March 14, 2016. http://edition.cnn.com/2014/02/13/world/africa/cocoa-nomics-explained-infographic/index.html.

"Cocoa's Bitter Child Labour Ties." *BBC*, March 24, 2010, sec. Panorama. http://news.bbc.co.uk/panorama/hi/front_page/newsid_8583000/8583499.stm.

Coe, Sophie D., and Michael D. Coe. *The True History of Chocolate*. Third edition. London: Thames & Hudson, 2013.

Cuvelier, Paule, and Cathy Selena. *The History of Chocolate*. Paris: Flammarion, 2007.

"Direct Cacao." Accessed March 14, 2016. http://www.directcacao.org/.

"Divine Chocolate." *Divine Chocolate*. Accessed July 11, 2016. http://www.divinechocolate.com/us/.

Esquivel, Laura. *Like Water for Chocolate: A Novel in Monthly Installments, with Recipes, Romances, and Home Remedies*. 1st ed. New York: Doubleday, 1992.

Frydenborg, Kay. *Chocolate: Sweet Science and Dark Secrets of the World's Favorite Treat*. Boston: Houghton Mifflin Harcourt, 2015.

Greenspan, Karen. *The Timetables of Women's History: A Chronology of the Most Important People and Events in Women's History*. New York: Simon & Schuster, 1994.

Grun, Bernard, and Werner Stein. *The Timetables of History: A Historical Linkage of People and Events*. 4th ed. New York: Simon & Schuster, 2005.

"Hershey Community Archives | Ration D Bars." Accessed July 27, 2016. http://www.hersheyarchives.org/essay/details.aspx?EssayId=26.

"How Did Aztec Society Measure Wealth? • /r/AskHistorians." *Reddit*. Accessed January 8, 2016. https://www.reddit.com/r/AskHistorians/comments/3as1tv/how_did_aztec_society_measure_wealth/csfj68o?context=3.

"How Fair Is Fairtrade Chocolate?" *Chocablog*. Accessed March 14, 2016. http://www.chocablog.com/features/how-fair-is-fairtrade-chocolate/.

"How Sweet It Is — or Isn't: Finding Chocolate's Fountain of Health." Accessed March 14, 2016. http://www.cbc.ca/news/health/chocolate-health-myth-dissolves-1.2879898.

Inness, Sherrie A., ed. *Pilaf, Pozole, and Pad Thai: American Women and Ethnic Food*. Amherst: University of Massachusetts, 2001.

"Introducing the Big Consumer Boycott That Didn't Happen: Quaker Chocolate and the São Tomé Cocoa Scandal 1902-9." *Chomping at the Bloodied Bit*, October 5, 2012. https://hughcrosfield.wordpress.com/2012/10/05/introducing-the-dog-that-didnt-bark-in-the-night-time-quaker-chocolate-and-the-sao-tome-cocoa-scandal-1902-9/.

Lee, Wan-chen Jenny, Mitsuru Shimizu, Kevin M. Kniffin, and Brian Wansink. "You Taste What You See: Do Organic Labels Bias Taste Perceptions?" *Food Quality and Preference* 29, no. 1 (July 2013): 33–39. doi:10.1016/j.foodqual.2013.01.010.

Macdonald, Kate, and Shelley Marshall, eds. *Fair Trade, Corporate Accountability and beyond: Experiments in Globalizing Justice*. Farnham, Surrey, England; Burlington, Vt: Ashgate, 2010.

Nall, Jeff. "Combating Slavery in Coffee and Chocolate Production." *Toward Freedom*. Accessed March 23, 2016. http://www.towardfreedom.com/35-archives/labor/2601-combating-slavery-in-coffee-and-chocolate-production.

"Novelty Chocolate Recipes." Ask MetaFilter, May 9, 2014. http://ask.metafilter.com/261654/Novelty-Chocolate-Recipes

Purt, Jenny. "Empowering Smallholder Farmers to Create Sustainable Change - Live Discussion." *The Guardian*, February 25, 2013, sec. Guardian Sustainable Business. http://www.theguardian.com/sustainable-business/empowering-smallholder-farmers-sustainable-change-live-discussion.

Robbins, John. "The Good, the Bad and the Savory." Earth Island Institute. 2002. Accessed April 11, 2017. Earthisland.org/journal/index.php/eij/article/the_good_the_bad_and_the_savory/.

Rosenblum, Mort. *Chocolate: A Bittersweet Saga of Dark and Light*. 1st ed. New York: North Point Press, 2005.

Ruy Sánchez, Alberto, Margarita de Orellana, and Artes de México, eds. *Chocolate: cultivo y cultura del México antiguo*. Artes de México, 103.2011. México, DF: Artes de México, 2011.

Satre, Lowell J. Chocolate on Trial: Slavery, Politics, and the Ethics of Business. Ohio University Press, 2005.

Skwarecki, Beth. "Chocolate Is Not a Superfood (but It's Still Super)." *Vitals*. Accessed March 14, 2016. http://vitals.lifehacker.com/chocolate-is-not-a-superfood-but-its-still-super-1684007178.

"Superfood 'Ban' Comes into Effect." *BBC*, June 29, 2007, sec. Health. http://news.bbc.co.uk/2/hi/health/6252390.stm.

"Sweet Remedy: Chocolate Can Help You Beat Persistent Coughs." *Mail Online*, December 8, 2012. http://www.dailymail.co.uk/health/article-2245042/Chocolate-help-beat-persistent-coughs.html.

"The Good, the Bad and the Savory." Global Exchange. Accessed March 14, 2016. http://www.globalexchange.org/news/good-bad-and-savory.

"The Great Boycott That Didn't Happen: Drinking Cocoa and the Absence of a São Tomé Blood-Cocoa Topos." *Chomping at the Bloodied Bit*, October 12, 2012. https://hughcrosfield.wordpress.com/2012/10/12/the-great-boycott-that-didnt-happen-drinking-cocoa-and-the-absence-of-a-sao-tome-blood-cocoa-topos/.

"The Problem with Fair Trade Coffee (SSIR)." Accessed March 13, 2016. http://ssir.org/articles/entry/the_problem_with_fair_trade_coffee.

Trips, Africa. "Ten Reasons Why the Ivorian Cocoa Farmer Is Poor: 3. Ten Factors That Have Contributed to the Impoverishment of the Ivorian Cocoa Farmer." *Ten Reasons Why the Ivorian Cocoa Farmer Is Poor*, September 22, 2010. http://ivoriancocoafarmer.blogspot.com/2010/09/3-ten-factors-that-have-contributed-to.html.

Tunnell, Michael O. *Candy Bomber: The Story of the Berlin Airlift's "Chocolate Pilot."* Watertown, MA: Charlesbridge, 2010.

"When Chocolate Was Medicine: Colmenero, Wadsworth and Dufour." *The Public Domain Review*. Accessed April 26, 2016. /2015/01/28/when-chocolate-was-medicine-colmenero-wadsworth-and-dufour/.

Wilson, Philip K., and W. Jeffrey Hurst. *Chocolate as Medicine: A Quest over the Centuries*. Cambridge, UK: RSC Pub, 2012.

SUBSCRIBE TO EVERYTHING WE PUBLISH!

Do you love what Microcosm publishes?

Do you want us to publish more great stuff?

Would you like to receive each new title as it's published?

Subscribe as a BFF to our new titles and we'll mail them all to you as they are released!

$10-30/mo, pay what you can afford. Include your t-shirt size and your birthday for a possible surprise!

microcosmpublishing.com/bff

...AND HELP US GROW YOUR SMALL WORLD!

Read more about the Food Revolution:

  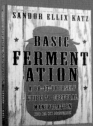